The Make It Fun Guide to *Romeo and Juliet*

By Larry K. Hartsfield, Ph.D.

Copyright 2013
Wolfdancer Publishing
Durango, CO 81301

Printed in the United States of America

1st Edition

ISBN: 978-0-9839190-5-6

Hartsfield, Larry K. The Make It Fun Guide to *Romeo and Juliet*/ Larry Hartsfield

The Make It Fun Guide to Romeo and Juliet

Dedication

This book is dedicated to my grandsons, Guthrie, Dexter, and Sowah, and their passion for life and learning;

and to all those who devote themselves to continued learning and a search for understanding;

and, as always, to Ellen, whose editorial skills and insights make my life and my writing better than either could ever be alone.

The Make It Fun Guide to Romeo and Juliet

Table of Contents

1. Introduction: The Make It Fun Guide to *Romeo and Juliet* 9

2. General Strategies for Reading Shakespeare 11

3. Shakespeare and His World 15

4. Shakespeare's Work: An Overview 21

5. Shakespeare's English 25

6. The Elizabethan World View 33

7. Shakespeare's Theater 43

8. *Romeo and Juliet* 45

9. Dramatis Personae or The Cast and Character Analysis 47

10. Background and Sources 55

11. Scene Synopsis and Analysis 57

12. Themes 97

13. Language and Poetic Conventions 111

14. Imagery 121

15. Activities 129

16. Film and Romeo and Juliet 141

Suggestions for Further Reading and Exploration 147

The Make It Fun Guide to Romeo and Juliet

Introduction:

The Make It Fun Guide to *Romeo and Juliet*

Welcome to the *Make It Fun Guide to Romeo and Juliet*. Whether you are a student, a teacher, a lover of Shakespeare productions, or just someone who would like to develop a better understanding and appreciation of Shakespeare, this book, and the Shakespeare *Make It Fun* series, were developed with you in mind. Shakespeare's plays continue to be the most-often staged plays in the world, and scarcely a year passes without another major Hollywood film based on a Shakespeare play. In spite of Shakespeare's continuing popularity, too often he is presented as difficult and overly serious—many people miss the humor and playfulness to be found in Shakespeare. Unfortunately, far too many students who approach a Shakespeare play such as *Romeo and Juliet* for the first time see reading the play as little more than a task to be accomplished, as an item to be checked off of a to-do list rather than something entertaining and enjoyable.

The purpose of this comprehensive guide is to make the play accessible, interesting, and meaningful. This in-depth guide to *Romeo and Juliet* includes a biography of Shakespeare, a presentation of the Elizabethan "worldview," a discussion of Shakespeare's use of language, as well as detailed analyses of characters, plot, themes, imagery, and the language of the play. This guide also includes a set of strategies for reading Shakespeare in the most effective way. Since movies are such an important part of today's culture, we also discuss films based on *Romeo and Juliet*. This guide presents a variety of activities to make experiencing *Romeo and Juliet* interactive, engaging, and educational.

Shakespeare is one of the funniest writers in English, yet we often forget that and put both the writer and his works on a pedestal. This guide is designed to recognize Shakespeare's genius but also to bring his work into easy reach for all of us—and that's who Shakespeare wrote his plays to entertain. Who was Shakespeare's audience in his own day? Everyone made up Shakespeare's audience—from the Queen, or later the King, to the lowliest members of society, known as the "groundlings," or those who stood on the ground around the stage. In fact, scholars estimate that in Shakespeare's day, one-third of all men in London saw his hit plays. Why more men than women? The men had more money and more freedom, but his plays were popular with all segments of society, just as they are today.

Our suggestions are that you use this guide in whatever ways you find most helpful. If you're interested in background on Shakespeare and his time, read that material first. If you're mostly interested in character, plot, or theme, read those sections. If you feel comfortable with the play, skip ahead to the activities. Our basic premise is that the cliché, "No pain, no gain," is horribly wrong. Learning about anything, but especially a subject as wonderful as Shakespeare, should be a fun process, never a painful one. *

---

* All quotations from Shakespeare are taken from *The Riverside Shakespeare*, 2nd edition, edited by Evans, G. Blakemore, Tobin, J.J. M, Herschel Baker, et al., New York: Houghton Mifflin Company, 1997.

General Strategies for Reading Shakespeare

The first thing to concentrate on when reading Shakespeare is not to worry about it. Approaching Shakespeare with fear or anxiety can become a self-fulfilling prophecy. In spite of the occasional strange spelling, his language isn't that different from what we speak today. Reading Shakespeare is challenging for everyone, but it can also be an adventure. Also, try to remember that there is no "correct" way to read Shakespeare. Here are some ideas that can make reading Shakespeare a bit easier.

1. Keep the list of the cast members handy so that you aren't constantly going back to the beginning of the play to see who's who. You might even want to make a copy of the cast list, so it's easily accessible as you read.

2. Try reading some passages out loud to get a sense of the language. This can be especially useful with soliloquies—those times when one character has a long "inner" speech that allows the audience to know what the character is thinking.

3. Use your imagination as you read. Try to think about how a character might deliver his lines, and how the meaning might change if the speech were delivered in a different way. Imagine the lines being spoken with different voices by the different characters. These are plays, and they were written to be performed, so use your imagination to supply things like special effects.

4. Watch a version of the play on television or on the stage. This can open up new dimensions to the play and its characters that you hadn't considered before. I recommend turning on the subtitles so that you can "read" the play as you watch a film version on television. Many different versions of Shakespeare's plays are available on DVD or through instant rental services for your television.

5. Try imagining people you know as the characters; how might one of your friends work as Romeo or Juliet or Mercutio? How would this friend deliver the lines?

6. Try to summarize a scene when you finish it. Use your own words. What were the key events that took place? Were any new characters introduced? Write down two or three memorable lines from the scene. Find an example of the language that is memorable, funny, or inventive.

7. Try to appreciate the humor in Shakespeare—it's everywhere.

8. Be flexible and open as you read. Try to be alert to the music of the language and to such things as rhyme. Also think about such things as the ways Shakespeare uses puns and the other ways he plays with language.

9. Finally, concentrate as fully as possible when you are reading, and if you find your mind drifting, go back and reread those passages. It's important to be willing to reread

passages that you find difficult and spend the time to understand them.

Shakespeare and His World

Shakespeare's early plays, including *Romeo and Juliet*, were written during the Elizabethan period. This period is known as the Elizabethan Age in Britain because of the powerful influence of Queen Elizabeth I, who was known as the Virgin Queen and for whom the state of Virginia in the United States is named. Queen Elizabeth was a powerful ruler but was also interested in the arts and scholarship. She was a poet who spoke six languages, a supporter of the theater, and a military strategist whose leadership helped defeat the powerful Spanish Armada in 1588. After her death in 1603, King James I became the King of England, Scotland, and Wales. The period when James I was king is known today as the "Jacobean" period, although the term "Elizabethan" is also used as a general term for the period that spanned their reigns. James I was so pleased with Shakespeare's acting group that he sponsored them, and they became known as The King's Men.

Despite all of the talk about the mystery of Shakespeare's life and all of the manufactured controversy over whether or not William Shakespeare wrote the plays he is credited with, Shakespeare is actually one of the better-known figures of the Elizabethan period and we have a number of documents relating to his life. These historical documents include not only the plays but also a variety of legal and religious documents. In spite of the documents and the plays, however, Shakespeare (like practically all Elizabethans) remains a mysterious figure in his personal life. This "mystery" has given rise to enormous amounts of speculation about his life, his marriage, and his personal relationships, and various biographers have chosen to emphasize different aspects of Shakespeare's lives. All of these biographies are, however, highly speculative and frequently reveal more about the biographer than about Shakespeare himself. That is, they involve guesswork and a heavy dose of imagination on the part of the biographer. If you're interested in pursuing more information about Shakespeare's life, some good starting points are Stephen Greenblatt's *Will and the World,* James Shapiro's *A Year in the Life of William Shakespeare*, and Jonathan Bate's *Soul of the Age.*

We know some facts about Shakespeare. Shakespeare was born in 1564 in Stratford-upon-Avon in England. His traditional birthdate, and death date as well, is April 23, which is also the name day for England's patron saint, Saint George. Shakespeare was baptized on April 26, 1564. His parents were John Shakespeare, a glover and leather merchant, and Mary Arden. William was the third of eight children, although three of these children died in childhood, an unfortunate yet common feature of life at this time. Shakespeare's father was, at the time of Shakespeare's birth, a successful merchant and local politician. He served as an alderman as well as High Bailiff of Stratford when William was young. In the late 1570s John Shakespeare's success began to decline, and he never recovered his earlier business success, a fact which led to Shakespeare having to leave school at the age of fourteen.

Although we know very little of Shakespeare's childhood, most scholars conclude that as a child he

The Make It Fun Guide to Romeo and Juliet

attended the free grammar school in Stratford. He would have been entitled to attend without paying tuition as a result of his father's work as a Stratford "official," and the Stratford free grammar school had an excellent reputation. Shakespeare's knowledge of Latin and, to a much smaller degree, classical Greek, support this idea. Roman writers and stories from Rome surface over and over in Shakespeare's writing, and the writer he drew most frequently upon for his plots was the Roman writer Ovid and his book, *Metamorphoses*. Shakespeare was intimately acquainted with other Latin classics and such Roman playwrights as Plautus and Seneca, both of whom were powerful influences on his early plays. Shakespeare did not attend a university, and this lack of extended formal education was at times an issue in his life.

Shakespeare's marriage to Anne Hathaway took place on November 28, 1582. At the time Anne was 26 and William was 18. Anne was also pregnant and their first child, Susanna, was born six months after the marriage. Three years later, in 1585, Anne gave birth to the twins, Hamnet and Judith, although Hamnet died at the age of 11 in 1596.

After the birth of Hamnet and Judith, Shakespeare disappears from any documentary records for seven years and is next referred to in London in 1592. This seven year period is often referred to as the "lost years" and has been the subject of enormous speculation such as whether or not he had to flee Stratford as a result of poaching (illegally killing game animals) a deer or whether he spent this time as a schoolteacher in some place other than Stratford such as in Lancashire.

Most scholars think Shakespeare came to London around 1588 and began to work as an actor and playwright almost immediately. Certainly he had written plays by 1592, at the age of 28, since he was attacked by the London playwright Robert Greene in his 1592 book, *A Groatsworth of Wit* as "… an upstart crow, beautified with our feathers, that with his Tiger's heart wrapped in a player's hide, supposes he is as well able to bombast out a blank verse as the best of you: and being an absolute *Johannes fac totum*, is in his own conceit the only Shake-scene in a country." In short, Greene didn't like Shakespeare or his work.

We know that by 1594 Shakespeare was acting and writing for the Lord Chamberlain's Men; after James I became king in 1603, this acting company, now called The King's Men, was clearly the leading theatrical company in England. In 1594 The Lord Chamberlain's men included the superb comedian Will Kempe, who would later be replaced by Robert Armin, and the leading tragic actor of the time, Richard Burbage. Shakespeare's company was popular, and Shakespeare was clearly one of the most successful playwrights of the period.

One of the reasons we know Shakespeare was popular is because of the number of his plays that were published as books. Scholars estimate that more than 3,000 plays were performed on the Elizabethan and Jacobean stage, and fewer than 650 of these have survived in printed versions. Only the most successful plays were turned into books. Shakespeare's plays were also the first plays by a single author to be collected and organized, after his death, into one complete edition, known today as the First Folio. If you want to experience Shakespeare's work as it was printed and appeared during his own period, do an internet search for the First Folio and explore some of the results. You can also download free versions of the First Folio to read on a tablet, computer, or smart phone, but be prepared—these will be very different in appearance from the Shakespeare you're used to reading.

When Shakespeare "retired" in 1611 he was a wealthy man, but even during his retirement he continued to collaborate with John Fletcher on plays such as *The Two Noble Kinsmen* for The King's Men. Shakespeare died on April 23, 1616 and was buried in Holy Trinity Church in Stratford on April 25, 1616. He left a short verse for his epitaph:

Good friend, for Jesus's sake forbeare

To dig the dust enclosed here.

Blessed be the man that spares these stones,

And cursed be he that moves my bones.

Perhaps the most important thing to keep in mind about Shakespeare is that he was born into a world that was experiencing huge change. The enormous shift occurring during the Elizabethan era makes itself felt in every aspect of Shakespeare's writings. Philosophically, the world Shakespeare entered at birth was essentially that of the Middle Ages; the world he left at his death was an early version of the modern world that all of us inhabit. Even though at times Shakespeare's world may seem foreign to the modern reader, at other times the world is all too familiar. This era, known as the Renaissance, was one of the most creative times in human history and shaped our contemporary world through its combination of older religious belief systems with such modern issues as the rise of science, the rise of secular thinking, printing, the exploration of new lands, the beginnings of capitalism, a rebirth of interest in the classical learning of Greece and Rome, and changing concepts of what it means to be a human, an individual, a self—questions that go to the very heart of identity. Some scholars, such as Harold Bloom, have argued that in his plays Shakespeare invented what it means to be a modern human, and many have argued that the character of Hamlet is the ultimate expression of what it means to be a thinking and deeply feeling human in the modern world.

Even though at times it might seem difficult to inhabit the ways of looking at the world and the ways of living that were central to Shakespeare, the rewards of this attempt are great. It also helps to remember that even though we live four centuries after Shakespeare, we share many things with him and his age such as a sense of an individual, or personal, destiny, an awareness of our world as a globe filled with diversity, and a value placed on education, poetry, and the arts.

Shakespeare's Work: An Overview

Shakespeare was the most popular playwright of his time even though the Elizabethan Age produced many other great playwrights such as Christopher Marlowe and Ben Jonson. Shakespeare's plays fall into four general time periods in his life. These periods are:

Before1594: This is the period when Shakespeare was learning his craft and includes such plays as the comedies *The Taming of the Shrew, The Comedy of Errors, Two Gentlemen of Verona*, the history plays treating Henry the Sixth, and the tragedies *Titus Andronicus, and Richard III. Richard III* is often considered one of the history plays today. During this early period of learning his craft, Shakespeare drew heavily upon the Roman plays he studied in school. The tragedies *Titus Andronicus* and *Richard III* also show just how important an influence the works of his contemporary, Christopher Marlowe, were to Shakespeare. Shakespeare learned many of his lessons about writing from Marlowe's plays such as *Dr. Faustus,* and *The Jew of Malta.*

1594-1600: During this second period Shakespeare's work shows growth in style, construction, and character development. Shakespeare's history plays of this period, which include the Henry the Fourth plays as well as *King John*, *Richard the Second,* and *Henry V,* are his best in this genre. This is also the period during which he wrote *Romeo and Juliet*, *Julius Caesar*, and the comedies *A Midsummer Night's Dream* and *The Merchant of Venice.* During this period Shakespeare began to mix tragedy and comedy in the same play, and this blending becomes one of his stylistic trademarks. Shakespeare's ability to create memorable characters becomes much more pronounced during this time.

1600-1608: This is the period that saw the writing of Shakespeare's great tragedies, *Hamlet, Othello, King Lear*, and *Macbeth*, as well as the comedies known as the "problem plays." The "problem plays," or "dark comedies," are cynical and often bleak. These include *Troilus and Cressida, All's Well That Ends Well,* and *Measure for Measure.* During this period Shakespeare reached the height of his power, and his characters in the great tragedies equal or surpass those of such writers as Euripides and Sophocles from the classical Greek tradition. The problem plays reveal, however, that Shakespeare was having difficulty writing light-hearted comic plays. These plays often lack a traditional comic resolution and can seem moody and bitter at times.

After 1608: Shakespeare turned to writing a completely new kind of play for him. These are the plays known today as the romances. These plays include *Pericles, Cymbeline, The Winter's Tale,* and *The Tempest.* During Shakespeare's own time, these were referred to as tragicomedies since they included elements associated with both tragedy and comedy. These plays show a preoccupation with the themes of forgiveness and redemption and are the most highly symbolic of Shakespeare's plays. The writing is often serious and can be difficult for readers, but these plays also contain some of Shakespeare's most intriguing writing. Some critics and scholars argue that these romances should be understood as the work of a writer nearing the end of his life and trying to find closure and meaning in his relationships and in his life.

Shakespeare's English

Today English is a global powerhouse of a language and is the native language of hundreds of millions of people and the second language of many, many more, but this wasn't true in the sixteenth century. At that time English was the language of only a few million people living on an isolated island that had been dominated by Norman French-speaking conquerors after 1066. English wasn't even the native language of all people in Great Britain. Welsh Gaelic dominated the western part of the island, and Scots Gaelic dominated the northern part. English itself was a collection of dialects which speakers from different areas often found to be incomprehensible. For example, some English dialects still used the word "eyren" to mean what we call "eggs." Regional differences in English were much greater than they are today, and neither spelling nor grammar had been standardized. A writer might spell the same word two or three different ways in his work. Conventions that we use today about how to punctuate a sentence or about not ending a sentence with a preposition had not yet been invented and made part of our speech and writing. English was, at this time, an extraordinarily fluid and flexible language, and this gave Shakespeare the freedom to create the many, many new words (called neologisms) that he added to our language. Although not all the words he coined caught on, Shakespeare is credited with introducing such words as "eyeball," "swagger," "zany," and "obscene" to English. He also used words in new ways. "Blanket" had long been a noun in English, but Shakespeare is credited as being the first writer to use "blanketed" as a verb.

During Shakespeare's life, however, English started to be regularized as a result of printing. William Caxton introduced the printing press to England in 1476, and printing quickly became the most important method of reproducing texts and language. As Robert McCrum (2002) and others point out, the introduction of printing created a communications revolution that has not been matched until the present time with the introduction of computers, word processing, and the Internet. Between 1500 and 1640, more than 20,000 items in English were printed; this surge in printed materials contributed to the increasing importance of education and the spread of literacy in England. Estimates suggest that about half of the population of England living in towns and cities had at least minimal literacy by 1600. Printing increased standardization in many areas such as spelling, although personal spellings continued to be used in private writing. Six examples of William Shakespeare's signature exist, and he spelled "Shakespeare" in different ways in these signatures.

The printing press tended to freeze language in a standard, or correct, form. Still, there were no dictionaries or formal grammars in Shakespeare's time. The first "dictionary" in English was Robert Cawdrey's *A Table Alphabeticall*, which appeared in 1604 and was little more than a list of words. Cawdrey's book included only 2,521 words and concentrated on so-called "hard" words—words that were new to English at the time. It's also worth recalling that Shakespeare would have primarily studied Latin, and perhaps a little classical Greek, but not English when he was a schoolboy. The formal study of English didn't become part of the educational system until the nineteenth century.

Shakespeare's command of language is the most striking feature of his plays, and much of this is due to his own flexible approach to language. He was never afraid to invent words or to use words in new ways. The *Oxford English Dictionary* credits Shakespeare with having introduced more than 2,000 words into the language, and Shakespeare's written vocabulary was well over 21,000 words. As Louis Marder notes, "Shakespeare was so facile in employing words that he was able to use over 7,000 of them—more than occur in the whole King James version of the Bible—only once and never again." We could also compare Shakespeare's control of language with the greatest French playwright of the Renaissance, Racine, whose written vocabulary included approximately 2,000 words.

How does Shakespeare's vocabulary compare to the average speaker of English today? Robert McCrum estimates that the average educated person who speaks English today has an active vocabulary of about 15,000 words. David Crystal has a very different thought. Crystal points out that the vocabulary of English has grown from about 150,000 words during Shakespeare's time to over 600,000 words today, and Crystal estimates that most educated speakers of English today have a vocabulary of over 50,000 words—twice as large as Shakespeare's (Crystal, 3). The truth is certainly somewhere in between these estimates, but the key thing to remember is that it is the *quality* of Shakespeare's language, not the quantity of words he used, that created his lasting influence on the language.

Shakespeare's English is still very similar to the English we speak today. Linguists refer to the English of Shakespeare's time as Early Modern English, and it is only one linguistic generation away from what we speak and write today. Even though the Elizabethan dialect has some differences from contemporary English, the principles and rules are basically the same. Some of Shakespeare's words have shifted meanings and some may seem odd to us, but his language is still relatively easy for us to make sense of although a word such as "wherefore" in *Romeo and Juliet* may give us pause until we realize that for Shakespeare "wherefore" simply meant "why."

Early Modern English was, however, more flexible than Modern English in the areas of grammar, spelling, and punctuation. Grammar, spelling, and punctuation help people make sense of language, and the ways a language puts words into patterns to create meaning. The grammatical standards for English have not changed much during the last 400 years. David Crystal points out that "90 percent of the word-orders and word formations used by Shakespeare are still in use today" (p. 178). Still, there were differences. For example, it was still acceptable in Early Modern English to use double negatives, such as "I don't have none," and double comparatives like "that's the most best sandwich I ever had. N.F. Blake (2006) points out that these constructions were later regarded as illogical "because in Latin two negatives make a positive and because you cannot have the 'most' of something which is already superlative" (p. 72).

Verbs are one kind of word that demonstrate linguistic change. For example, an older form of the third person verb that was still present in Early Modern English was the ending *–eth*, so rather than say, as we do today, "she moves," Shakespeare might write, "she mov*eth*." Another example is in the verb form ending in *-est* associated with the second person singular pronoun *thou* (which itself has disappeared from the language) as in "thou think*est*" instead of "you think." *Inflections* are endings added to words that indicate things such as singular or plural (the "s" added to word "dog*s*), or verb tense (the "ed" added to the word "walk*ed* to make the past tense form of the verb. Inflections in English also indicate whether the subject of a verb is in the first person (I or we), second person (you), or third person (he, she, it, or they). In both instances of verb forms above (mov*eth* and think*est*) an *inflection* has been dropped

28

from the way we use the word today, and this dropping of inflections is characteristic of the linguistic changes taking place in Early Modern English.

The loss of inflections represents a simplification of English grammar and had important impacts on Modern English. As the endings dropped away from many words, word order became more important than inflections in clarifying the meaning of sentences and in creating structure in English.

This simplification can also be seen in the loss of the informal form of the second person pronoun, "thou." This simple word, and its friends such as "thee," is such a central feature of the language of Shakespeare that one often encounters speakers today who make use of these pronouns to create the "atmosphere" of an earlier time—just visit any Renaissance Faire today. The *thou* forms are *thou, thee, thy, thine,* and *thy selfe,* while the *you* forms are *you, ye, your, yours,* and *your selfe*. While the "thou" forms still occur in some regional dialects today, they have essentially disappeared from standard Modern English. These different forms of the second person pronoun, "you," are important in Early Modern English because they indicate such things as differences between social classes, an aspect of daily life at that time that has largely disappeared in our more democratic era. In Old English *thou* was the singular second person pronoun and *you,* or *ye,* was the plural form, and these pronouns did not indicate intimate relationships or social class, but during the thirteenth century, probably as a result of French influence, *thou* began to be used as the familiar or intimate form of the second person pronoun, and *you* began to be used as the formal version of the same pronoun. Thus, a speaker might address a servant or a child or an intimate companion or lover with *thou* while a servant might address a master or mistress with *you.* Shakespeare provides an example of this in a dialogue between Portia (the mistress) and Nerissa (the servant) in *The Merchant of Venice*:

> **Nerissa**: *Your* father was ever virtuous, and holy men at their death have good
> inspirations; therefore the lott'ry that he hath devis'd in these three chests of gold,
> silver, and lead, whereof who chooses his meaning chooses *you*, will no doubt
> never be chosen by any rightly but one who *you* shall rightly love. But what warmth is there in *your* affection towards any of these princely suitors that are
> already come?
> **Portia**: I pray *thee* over-name them, and as *thou* namest them, I will describe
> them; and according to my description level at my affection (1.2.27-38).

Portia is responding to the formal use of the word "you" with its informal equivalent "thou." Why are these different pronouns used? The servant had to be formal and polite, so she used the "you" form of the pronoun, while the "mistress," Portia, used the intimate or informal form. This use of "thou" instead of "you" establishes Portia's higher social status. "Thou" and its related forms also indicated that the speakers knew each other well. Family members, close friends, and lovers would typically use the word "thou."

Another example from *The Merchant of Venice* illustrates how the pronoun indicated distinction in social rank even during a heated argument such as this one between Shylock, who was Jewish and therefore of lower social status at the time, and Antonio, who was Venetian:

Shylock: 'Fair sir, *you* spet on me on Wednesday last,

You spurn'd me such a day, another time

You call'd me dog; and for these courtesies

I'll lend *you* thus much moneys"?

Antonio: I am as like to call *thee* so again,

To spet on *thee* again, to spurn *thee* to.

If *thou* wilt lend this money, lend it not

As to *thy* friends, . . .

But lend it rather to *thine* enemy," (1.3.126-137).

The disappearance of these forms and their replacement by *you* is an indication of the tendency to simplify grammar that marks the history of English. People today don't use these terms or might misuse them if they try, but the forms still remain familiar to us and are still used in prayer even today.

The Elizabethan World View

The Elizabethan period (1558-1603) was one of vibrant growth and change. During this period England became one of the leading military and economic powers in the world. Elizabeth I fostered exploration of "new" lands and firmly established the Church of England and its form of Protestantism as the religion of England. London was the center of the country and emerged as one of the cultural centers of the world. During the sixteenth century London grew at an enormous rate—a 400 percent increase in population with around 200,000 people living in London at the time Shakespeare arrived in the mid 1580s. This concentration of people contributed to the emergence of a new kind of drama during the Elizabethan era. When Shakespeare arrived in the 1580s the London theater was dominated by a group of writers known as the University Wits. These writers included Christopher Marlowe, Robert Greene, John Lyly, Thomas Kyd, and George Peele. Christopher Marlowe was the best of these writers, and his plays had an enormous influence on Shakespeare— especially Marlowe's powerful blank verse.

These writers were known as the University Wits because all of them were highly and formally educated. They had all attended university, a rarity at this time, and a mark of distinction. Shakespeare was considered an "outsider" by the University Wits and endured their occasional taunts at his lack of formal schooling and social status. Even today some people argue that a person as "uneducated" as Shakespeare could not really have written the plays that bear his name, and so they put forward other, more educated and socially distinguished people as the "true" Shakespeare. The recent movie, *Anonymous*, takes this stance. This denial of Shakespeare as the author of his works is usually based on little more than social snobbery. In The Make It Fun Series, we stand solidly behind Shakespeare as the writer, the brilliant writer, of his work.

The Elizabethan worldview, or basic assumptions about how the world works, can seem foreign to the modern reader, but many of its elements are still present in our culture today. One of the most important differences between the Elizabethans and our time is the way they knew "truth." The Elizabethans had a different "truth test" than most of us use today. Remember that this was a period of transition from a medieval/classical worldview to a modern one. Today our worldview is based on a scientific approach to the world, one that emphasizes personal experience, observation, and experimentation. Our truth is largely based on experience and can differ from one individual to the next. The Elizabethans primarily relied on a truth test known as "authority," even though this was changing as the scientific way of approaching the world became more and more common. The appeal to authority was based on what the ancient writers and the Bible said about the world. For the Elizabethans the strongest method of discovering "truth" was to appeal to those who had written before. Galen was the authority in medical practice, and physicians relied more heavily on what he said about disease and healing than on their own observations. Aristotle was the authority in natural philosophy, art, and rhetoric. If the Bible said that God stopped the sun to allow Joshua and his followers to have more time to destroy their enemies, then that was accepted as true. If an ancient historian such as the Greek writer, Herodotus, said that a species of men existed whose heads were located in the abdomen, rather than on top of the neck, then that was accepted as true—even if no one had yet encountered this kind of human.

The Elizabethans also had a world-view based on hierarchy and harmony (although recent scholars such as Thomas McAlindon have questioned just how strong this vision was). As Robert Browning had one of his characters state 300 years later, "God's in his heaven, all's right with the world." For the Elizabethans everything had its proper place, and if things were in harmonious balance, the world worked for everyone. This harmony and balance, however, were constantly threatened by disharmony and chaos, and that points to another aspect of the Elizabethan world view—polarity or opposition. Although Copernicus and Galileo had already put forward a vision of the universe that pictured the earth revolving around the sun (heliocentric), most Elizabethans continued to conceive of the universe in the model described by the Greek philosopher Ptolemy, which is known as the Ptolemaic world-view. In this vision Earth was the center of the universe, and the sun, moon, and planets revolved around the Earth in concentric spheres or circles. Outside the spheres of the planets was the sphere of the fixed stars (those that we use to create constellations) and beyond the fixed stars was the world of God, Heaven. Everything was orderly and when one was in tune with the world, one could even hear the music created by these various spheres as they revolved—a music that Lorenzo in *The Merchant of Venice* refers to and hears. This is the universe in harmony, the universe as it should be.

The same vision of order found in the heavens applies to life on earth. God created humans at the center of the earthly world, and God meant for humans to rule over the world and all other creatures. Government followed this same pattern with the King or Queen at the top of the hierarchy, who are clearly blessed by God since they are the ones in power. Below the monarch are the various degrees and ranks of the larger society. The king is God's representative on earth, but a good king also rules by law and does not make justice dependent on his own whims or will. The laws of God justify hereditary right. The ruler must care for his subjects, just as a father cares for his children and the subjects owe their king the same love and obedience that children owe their father. Even bad kings rule by God's choice, and it is up to God, not the subjects, to remove him. In God's own time, the tyrant will die. An evil ruler might be a punishment for the sins of the people. However, the king's authority is divinely sanctioned and actions such as rebellion or treason are the equivalent of atheism or an arrogant pride that assumes humans know better than God.

History is an important part of this worldview and is central to the tragic vision of a play such as *Romeo and Juliet*. The classical view of tragedy always involves the fall of a great individual from a high place in society. Clearly, this isn't the case for *Romeo and Juliet* which features two teen-agers thwarted in love. Shakespeare often takes a more medieval view of history which emphasizes "Fortune" and "The Wheel of Fortune" which constantly circles and sometimes places the individual at the top with good luck and good things happening and sometimes at the bottom with the character's world falling apart. It's no accident that after slaying Tybalt, Romeo exclaims, "Oh, I am Fortune's fool." The important concept here is the instability of human fortune—we are all subject to periods where we go up as well as periods where we go down, and we have no control over this.

On Earth, however, there is an important difference from all the rest of the universe and that is the concept of *mutability*, of change, of time. The rest of the universe is eternal and unchanging like God, but humans, because they sinned in the Garden of Eden, inhabit a world of change, of death, of time—of mutability. Even though the new Copernican vision of the universe was becoming more widely accepted during the Elizabethan era, it's important to remember that Shakespeare often uses the older vision of the universe as a place of order. Shakespeare's primary concerns are always humanity and society and the imperfect nature of these on earth. This conflict between order and disorder is a major element in *Romeo and Juliet*. The play opens in disorder and immediately the Prince tries to assert order through his commands. Human nature, however, doesn't always work in orderly ways and that disorder is at the center of both plot and theme in *Romeo and Juliet*. The fathers in this play continually try to impose authority and order on their children, especially Juliet, and this attempt to impose order on the anarchic energies of youth and love creates the tragedy of this play.

Another crucial aspect of the Elizabethan worldview is the elements. This vision of the elements making up everything in the universe comes from the classical world of the Greeks and the Romans. The Elizabethans conceived of the world and the universe as made up of four elements: earth, air, fire, and water. The idea of the elements was based on the concepts of hot, cold, dry, and moist. Imagery built on the concept of the elements is frequently part of Shakespeare's plays and is central to *Romeo and Juliet*. Each element has its own characteristics, and these characteristics are always made up of two qualities. For example, earth is conceived as cold and dry and is the most lumpish and heavy of the elements. It is easily altered by the superior elements of water, air, and fire and is the element most subject to mutability or change. Water was cold and moist and was considered "nobler" or higher than earth. Air was hot and moist and was nobler than water. Fire was hot and dry and was the noblest of all the elements. Even though the Elizabethans spoke of the elements as four different things, they conceived of them as almost always being mixed up together and struggling with the other elements for dominance. In an ideal and harmonious world, the elements would all be in balance, but that isn't the case in this world of change.

Perhaps the best explanation of the elements and how they work comes from one of Shakespeare's favorite writers, Ovid. Ovid's theme in his great book *Metamorphoses*, is change, transformation, or metamorphosis. In the last book of *Metamorphoses*, Ovid has the Greek philosopher, Pythagoras, explain the elements (this is from the modern translation of Ovid by David Raeburn):

"This law of impermanence also applies to what we call elements.

Pay attention, and I shall explain the changes they pass through.

The world eternal contains four bodies which generate matter.

Two of them, earth and water, are heavy and gravitate downwards;

the other two, air and fire, which is even purer, are weightless

and tend to make their way up, if nothing is pressing them down.

Although these elements occupy different positions in space,

they form the source and the end of all matter. When earth breaks up,

it is rarefied into water; the moisture is thinned still further and changes to wind and to air; which in time, relieved of its weight

and now as thin as can be, darts up to the fire in the ether.

The process is then unraveled, and all the elements change back:

fire is thickened and crosses again into denser air,

air forms into water, and water's compressed into firm, hard earth.

' " Nothing retains its original form, but Nature, the goddess

of all renewal, keeps altering one shape into another.

Nothing at all in the world can perish, you have to believe me;

things merely vary and change their appearance. What we call birth

is merely becoming a different entity; what we call death

is ceasing to be the same. Though the parts may possibly shift

their position from here to there, the wholeness in nature is constant

(*Metamorphoses*, Book 15, 237-258).

This vision of the elements extends to all areas of Elizabethan thought; a good way to illustrate this is to look at the theory of the humours. For the Elizabethans, humans are oddly contradictory creatures who have an immortal and eternal soul housed in a mutable body subject to illness, decay, and death. Humans are primarily distinguished by having the ability to reason and yet being caught in endless conflict between desire for the eternal, the perfect, the ideal, and the desires and appetites of the mutable body. This conflict in the world of humans inescapably leads to the problem of evil. The duality of humanity is central to the problem of evil. Paradoxically, the human soul is capable of knowing all things on earth except itself.

The body owes its sustenance to the four elements. The theory of the humours is a way of explaining everything from illness to psychology for the Elizabethans. Like the theory of the elements, the theory of the humours goes back to classical times and the ancient Greeks and Romans. The Greek physician, Hippocrates, first developed the theory of the humours into a medical theory and argued that certain human behaviors, moods, and illnesses were related to an imbalance of the fluids of the body.

Remember that each element has its own defining characteristics. When the humours are in proper balance, people are in good moods and health, but when one of the humours is excessive, a person falls into bad moods and illness. These moods and illnesses are connected to the humours and what they correspond to in the theory of the elements Sometimes the humours are referred to as the temperaments. The humours correspond to these elements and bodily fluids:

Melancholic is cold and dry like earth and is associated with the fluid, "black bile";

Phlegmatic is cold and moist like water, and is associated with the fluid, "phlegm";

Sanguine is hot and moist like air and is associated with the fluid "blood";

Choleric is hot and dry like fire, and is associated with the fluid, "yellow bile."

Eventually physicians identified nine different temperaments associated with the humours. The physician Galen identified the four most important as "melancholic," "sanguine," "choleric," and "phlegmatic." The melancholic person would often be depressed, but this humour was also associated with introversion, deep thought, deep sensitivity, moodiness, and creativity. Melancholics also had a strong tendency to procrastinate or put things off. The sanguine person was generally optimistic and what today would be called an extrovert. The sanguine humour was often associated with seeking pleasure as well as creativity. Self-confidence was also part of the sanguine temperament. The choleric temperament was often associated with ambition and leadership, but it was also aggressive and easily slipped into violence. Cholerics were often associated with anger. The phlegmatic was usually quiet but also relaxed, although this temperament was also associated with laziness and sluggishness. Phlegmatics were usually pretty happy with things as they were and with themselves. They were non-judgmental and could be shy. They also didn't like change.

In many ways the word "humour" came to mean a person's dominant mood. A brief summary of the humours and personalities would be that a melancholic person would be depressed; a phlegmatic person would be slow to act and difficult to arouse; a sanguine person would be optimistic and excitable; and a choleric person would be quick to anger and violence. One fascinating aspect of the humours is that different humours came in and out of fashion just like clothing or music. During the period when Shakespeare wrote, the most fashionable humour was melancholy. In addition to being depressed, melancholics were thought to be more sensitive than other people, more emotional. Lest we think this too strange, ask yourself if you know any one who presents themselves as "depressed" or more sensitive than others. The fairly recent trend in music known as "emo" and its associated style of behavior and dress call to mind the melancholic humour of the Renaissance.

Another thing to keep in mind is that most Elizabethans took astrology, or the influence of the stars on human destiny, seriously. This does not mean that humans lacked free will or the ability to shape their destiny. The prologue to *Romeo and Juliet* refers to the two main characters as "star-crossed lovers," but their fates are not inescapable. We all have the ability to influence and change our fate, and to a large extent this ability is based on being flexible and imaginative as well as our openness to change. The young lovers in *Romeo and Juliet* try to move beyond "destiny," and overcome such obstacles to their love as family enmity and the feud, but they are unable to overcome the rigidity of their society and their families. The difficulty of moving beyond the patterns of family and culture in which one grows up is especially evident in Act 3, Scene 1. Romeo and Juliet have just been married, and even though Tybalt tries to provoke Romeo into a duel, Romeo refuses to be drawn into a fight. However, once Tybalt kills Mercutio, Romeo falls into the rigid and inflexible rules of the honor code of his society as he seeks revenge for the death of Mercutio. After Tybalt's death, Romeo and Juliet are doomed, and their destiny becomes something almost impossible to escape, an inevitable consequence into which they will fall.

Shakespeare's Theater

As you read and think about *Romeo and Juliet* (or any other Shakespeare play), it's helpful to remember that watching a play during Shakespeare's time was very different from watching a play, a movie, or a television program today. We're used to lavish special effects—especially visual special effects. Setting or location is an important part of practically any kind of visual theater we see. Staged performances were very different during Shakespeare's time. These actors were working with essentially no special effects and very few props, if any. The stage itself was usually bare with no setting at all. These plays were also performed in an open-air setting during daylight, so there were no lighting effects. Even music was used differently. We're used to mood-setting music and background music with our films and television programs. Most of the actors during Shakespeare's time were able to play musical instruments, but these instruments were used to accompany songs during the performances or for the dances that usually followed a performance. Costumes were an important part of the onstage presentation of character and often these costumes were the greatest single expense of a theatrical company.

The most important consequence of this absence of the surrounding elements we consider central to the theatrical experience today is that it all came down to language and words. Words were used to set the mood, to set the scene, to give the audience information about setting, and to help the audience imagine things such as props. Language was the most central aspect in helping to create the illusions that all theater relies on. One more thing to keep in mind is that all of the actors in Shakespeare's day were male, and boys acted the female roles, such as Juliet.

Romeo and Juliet

Romeo and Juliet was most likely written around 1595-96, and ever since its first performance, it has been one of Shakespeare's most popular plays. At about the same time, Shakespeare wrote *A Midsummer Night's Dream*, which is a sort of companion piece to *Romeo and Juliet*, treating the same themes and even some of the same plot elements. Both plays are based on the classical story of Pyramus and Thisbe. The big difference between the two plays is that *A Midsummer Night's Dream* treats these themes and the story from a comic perspective, and everything works out well for everyone at the end. *Romeo and Juliet*, as you probably know, ends in the deaths of its heroes, the traditional ending for a tragedy.

Dramatis Personae or The Cast and Character Analysis

Escalus, Prince of Verona: Escalus represents authority and the attempt to impose order and rational behavior on disorder and irrationality. He is the ruler of Verona and both Mercutio and the County Paris are his kinsmen or relatives. He tries to force the warring families of the Montagues and the Capulets to cease their endless fighting and uses the threat of punishment to back it up. As often happens in Shakespeare, the figure representing authority is completely unable to bring the anarchic forces of humanity under control, and Escalus' voice for reason and moderation is not heeded by the warring families.

Paris, a young nobleman, kinsman to the Prince: Paris wants to marry Juliet, and although her father meets Paris' original proposal with the suggestion to wait a while, he eventually gives in to Paris' pleas and moves the marriage forward, thus setting in motion the final, tragic ending. Romeo kills Paris when both arrive at Juliet's tomb at the same time. Paris has tried to avoid being drawn into the feud between the two families, yet he dies as a result of the feud. Shakespeare is implying that these kinds of senseless feuds engulf everyone in a community—even those who try to stay apart from the quarrel and even those who, like Paris, are men of goodness and good will. "County" is a title for nobility such as "Count."

Montague, head of one of the two houses feuding with each other, and

Capulet, head of the other feuding house: These two fathers represent rigidity and the attempt to control change as well as the inability to move forward. As in many Shakespeare plays, attempts to control result in disaster. Here the fathers represent both the past, and their inability to visualize a future different from the one they currently inhabit, as well as the futility of attempts to control youthful energy, desire, and love.

An Old Man of the Capulet family makes a brief appearance.

Romeo, son to Montague: Romeo is a love-sick youth who has been infected by the Petrarchan tradition; at the beginning of the play he's more in love with the idea of being in love than in love with a specific woman, but during the course of the play he is transformed by the actual power of love into a true lover and a heroic figure. Our first vision of Romeo portrays him as a typical Petrarchan lover infatuated with Rosaline and speaking in the Petrarchan style which treated Rosaline as the unattainable and chaste love object. Romeo is much more interested in Rosaline than in the family feud, although he is eventually drawn into the feud and destroyed by it. Romeo's confidante and older advisor is Friar Lawrence. Romeo is a good example of the melancholic humor at the beginning of the play. After Romeo sees Juliet, his "love" for Rosaline completely disappears, and he falls utterly in love with Juliet. Shakespeare always uses language as an indicator of character and character development, and this is especially true with his development of Romeo. As the play progresses

Romeo moves farther and farther from the clichéd language of Petrarchanism and closer and closer to direct, plain speech. Romeo becomes more "real," more true to himself, and this honesty and forthright quality is reflected in how he speaks. After the secret marriage of Romeo to Juliet, he tries to stop the duel between Tybalt and Mercutio, only to accidentally bring about Mercutio's death. Romeo then kills Tybalt in revenge for the death of Mercutio. Romeo is, as Shakespeare writes, "fortune's fool."

Mercutio, kinsman to the Prince, and friend to Romeo: Mercutio is the source of the transformative power of the imagination in *Romeo and Juliet*; after his death at the beginning of Act 3, the play begins its unstoppable move toward tragedy. Mercutio's name identifies him as connected to Mercury, who was the messenger of the gods, as well as a mercurial, changeable, potentially transformative force. Mercutio is an example of the sanguine humor in this play. Mercutio is one of the only sources for potential change in *Romeo and Juliet*. He represents imagination and vision and dreams. Mercutio is also, paradoxically, a realist who doesn't accept the Petrarchan vision of love. He tries to get Romeo to take such things less seriously. His death represents the end of the possibility of change and pulls both Romeo and Juliet into the world of the feud between the two families.

Benvolio, nephew to Montague, and friend to Romeo: his name translates as "goodwill" and this is what he represents in the play. Benvolio is a young man who constantly tries to function as a peacemaker and to stop brawls and duels, but he is always unsuccessful in this endeavor.

Tybalt, nephew to Lady Capulet: a representative of irrational hatred as well as of the medieval honor code. Like the fathers, he is unable to see beyond the world he inhabits, a failure of vision that also infects Romeo after he has slain Tybalt with his comment, "There is no world beyond Verona's walls." Tybalt is a representative of the older world, the world of the honor code, and the world of revenge. He is hot-headed and always ready to fight.

Petruchio, a (mute) follower of Tybalt. Petruchio is mentioned by the Nurse when Juliet asks what Romeo's name is and is present later when Tybalt kills Mercutio.

Friar Lawrence, a Franciscan, advisor to Romeo: Friar Lawrence is the confessor to both Romeo and Juliet, but he is primarily Romeo's advisor and confidant. It is notable that both Romeo and Juliet have an older advisor (the Nurse is Juliet's), and that both of these advisors ultimately fail in providing good advice and leadership to the two young lovers. Romeo and Juliet are on their own in a difficult world. Our first meeting with Friar Lawrence shows that he has a wide knowledge of plants and the properties plants have either to heal or to harm. His monologue about plants opens Scene 3 of Act 2. This monologue is a clear example of Friar Lawrence's vision of the universe as harmonious and balanced as God intended. The play itself, however, undercuts this image of order and harmony. Friar Lawrence is a good man but proves ultimately unable to bring that goodness into a world of bitter hatred. He provides Juliet with the potion that will make her appear to be dead, and that leads to the eventual deaths of both Romeo and Juliet.

Friar John, a Franciscan: Friar John is told by Friar Lawrence to take letters to Romeo explaining that Juliet is not dead. He doesn't know how important the letters are and is delayed entering Mantua to deliver the letters because of fear of the plague, so that Romeo never receives the letters.

Balthasar, servant to Romeo: Balthasar is Romeo's servant and assists him in various ways. He brings the ladder to the Nurse that allows Juliet to leave her room; he also mistakenly tells Romeo that Juliet is dead.

Abram, servant to Montague: Abram is a servant to Montague and helps start the brawl that opens the play.

Sampson, servant to Capulet: Sampson is one of Capulet's servants whose language is filled with puns and bawdy. He also contributes to the opening brawl by "biting his thumb" at the Montague servants. Biting one's thumb at the time was the equivalent to an obscene gesture involving the middle finger that we all know well.

Gregory, servant to Capulet: Gregory also plays with words and contributes to the opening brawl by insulting the Montague servants.

Clown, servant to Capulet.

Peter, servant to Juliet's nurse: Peter goes with the Nurse when she meets Romeo in the public square. He also has a comic interaction with the musicians after Juliet's death.

Page, to Paris: Paris' servant who accompanies him to visit Juliet's grave.

Apothecary: essentially a pharmacist; he is a poor man living in Mantua (the city of Romeo's exile) who, in spite of the law forbidding it, sells Romeo a poison potion after Balthasar tells Romeo of Juliet's "death."

Three Musicians: these musicians play after Juliet's death and, oddly enough, serve as a source of humor during their interaction with Peter.

Lady Montague, wife to Montague and Romeo's Mother: Lady Montague tries to prevent her husband from joining the opening brawl. After Romeo is exiled, she dies of grief because of his banishment.

Lady Capulet, wife to Capulet and Juliet's Mother: Lady Capulet serves in some ways as a warning against the arranged or forced marriage that Capulet is determined to force upon Juliet. Lady Capulet is only about 28 years old. Juliet is almost fourteen and her mother refers to giving birth to Juliet when she was Juliet's age. She raises an interesting set of images when she broaches the subject of marrying Juliet to Paris. This set of images has to do with books and especially with the covers of the books and provides some insight into her lack of depth. She is devastated by the death of Tybalt, her nephew, and plans to poison Romeo in revenge. She is not a strong source of support for her daughter.

Juliet, daughter to Capulet: Juliet is one of Shakespeare's great tragic heroines even though she is still two weeks away from her fourteenth birthday when we meet her. When we first see her, she reveals herself as an obedient and dutiful daughter, but after she falls in love with Romeo, we see her passionate and headstrong side. Like Romeo, Juliet can play with the Petrarchan clichés as we see in the Balcony scene, but she doesn't take these seriously and sees through them. Juliet is direct and straightforward in her love and is willing to challenge her parents. She is also willing to take great risks for love. Juliet recognizes the physical aspect of love, and she looks forward to her wedding night. Her loyalty is demonstrated after the death of Tybalt—her immediate response is anger at Romeo, but she quickly refocuses on Romeo and her dismay over his exile. She demonstrates her courage in her willingness to use the potion provided by Friar Lawrence and to be buried alive in the Capulet tomb. Her devotion to Romeo is confirmed when she awakens in the tomb, finds Romeo dead, and immediately stabs herself with his dagger.

Nurse, to Juliet, and also her advisor: the Nurse is one of Shakespeare's great comic characters, but she is not as harmless as she might at first appear. In many ways the Nurse is a study in the bad effects of self-interest. The thing she's best at looking out for is herself, and she doesn't mind sacrificing Juliet if she thinks that will be better for herself (the Nurse) in the long run. Although she seems to put Juliet's interests first, her true self is revealed when she counsels Juliet to forget about her marriage to Romeo and to marry Paris. Just as Romeo's mentor, Friar Lawrence, fails him, the Nurse fails Juliet. One of the reasons the Nurse fails Juliet is that she is a static and unchanging character throughout the play. She exemplifies the inability to change and the destructiveness of this rigidity. The Nurse is presented very differently in the two halves of the play. In the first half of the play, which still has the possibility of a comic ending, the Nurse is humorous and charming. In the second, tragic, half of the play the Nurse is shown to be not only inadequate but also dangerous. In this shift the Nurse personifies the mood of the play. She is Juliet's closest advisor, and Juliet must have the self-knowledge to reject her advice. As a representative of the older generation, the Nurse is useless and must be rejected.

Citizens of Verona: these are various people who make up crowd scenes and the people at the parties and funerals.

Background and Sources

Romeo and Juliet is one of the most brilliant and complex depictions of love in literature. The play begins with "false" versions of love but moves from false or romantic conceptions of love and being in love to become what Harold Bloom has called, "The largest and most persuasive celebration of romantic love in Western literature." This play was the third tragedy that Shakespeare wrote (after *Titus Andronicus* between 1588 and 1593) and *Richard III* (around 1592). In both of the earlier tragedies Shakespeare concentrated on evil and suffering, but in this play he begins to ask profound questions about what it means to be human and what it means to love. *Romeo and Juliet* is a play that at first seems to lack the potential for high tragedy. The subject matter is two young lovers and their private lives as complicated by a meaningless family feud and parents trying to arrange marriages for their children. Indeed, the play seems to totter on the edge between tragedy and comedy until the death of Mercutio in Act 3 when it begins the relentless drive toward tragedy.

The story of Romeo and Juliet had been popular in England and Europe before Shakespeare used it as the basis for his play. The ultimate source for this story is the story of

Pyramus and Thisbe which Ovid tells in Book Four of *Metamorphoses*. Shakespeare knew Ovid, but he based his play primarily on a poem by Arthur Brooke, *The Tragical History of Romeus and Juliet* (1562). In Shakespeare's hands this plodding and dull poem was transformed into a play that shows us a brilliant vision of a love that is destroyed both by the demands of outside forces and by its own intensity. Arthur Brooke's poem is a translation/adaption of an earlier French work by Pierre Boaistuau originally published in Paris in 1559. Boaistuau's work was based on an Italian work by Mateo Bandello published in 1554 which in turn was based on another Italian work by Luigi Da Porto published in 1530. This tragic romance clearly captured the imaginations of writers and the public in the sixteenth century, but without Shakespeare's bold imagining of the story, we probably wouldn't know of it today.

Scene Synopsis and Analysis

Prologue: The play opens with a sonnet spoken by the chorus, which introduces both the subject of the play and several of the themes and image patterns, such as hands and blood, which will dominate the play. This play opens with a sonnet and Shakespeare uses several other sonnets during the course of the play. These sonnets contribute to the lyrical quality of *Romeo and Juliet*. The sonnet is a highly formalized poem with a strict rhyme pattern and meter. One of the things Shakespeare will explore in this play is the inability of "rules" to control or contain human behavior. The sonnet is traditionally a form devoted to poetry of love, yet this sonnet is devoted to irrational hatred and the tragedies that spring from irrational hatred. The opening sonnet brings up the themes of grudges, mutiny, violence, unrest, conflict between parents and children, and death. It also introduces the image patterns of blood, hands, ears, and astrology.

Act 1, Scene 1: The formal language and structure of the opening sonnet is immediately followed by anarchic prose, quarreling servants, and a riot in the streets of Verona which the Prince attempts to quell by imposing a rigid set of rules for the behavior of these two quarreling families—the Capulets and the Montagues. The opening of this scene is filled with Shakespeare's bawdy puns and humor. It also introduces the audience to the quarrel of the two families through the figures of Benvolio, Romeo's friend, and a Montague, and Tybalt, a Capulet. With Tybalt's entrance at line 65 the language of the scene shifts from prose to blank verse. Although Benvolio counsels peace, Tybalt forces him to fight. A brawl follows, and Prince Escalus ends the brawl with a strict prohibition on fighting, stating that whoever breaks the peace again will forfeit their lives.

The Prince's speech is notable for its introduction of the imagery of "beasts," the elemental imagery of "fire," and the imagery of "Cank'red with peace, to part your cank'red hate" (1.1.95). This imagery of "canker," which means cancer, will recur throughout the play and is used to depict something that is destroyed from the inside. Tybalt will frequently be associated with the element of fire, which is associated with "choler" and a choleric temperament—one that is always willing to fight and in which anger predominates.

Immediately after the riot is quelled, Lady Montague asks about Romeo, and Benvolio reveals to the audience that Romeo's temperament is one of melancholy, the perfect "humour" for a sensitive, romantic lead. Romeo enters the scene, and, in a conversation with Benvolio, we discover that Romeo is pining away for the love of Rosaline (or Rosalind). Romeo is a figure drenched in the traditions of courtly love and Petrarch, and during the course of the play he will discover the reality of love as opposed to the literary, "idealized" version of love (see the discussion of Petrarch below). Our first vision of Romeo is one of affectation, of a young man playing a part. He is in love with the idea of love rather than actually being in love, and he affects the fashionable humor of melancholy rather than accepting himself for who he is. Romeo is an actor playing a role rather than a real person living an authentic life.

Shakespeare frequently opens the plays from this period with an attempt by the older generation or a person in power to impose a rigid order on the forces of disorder (such as brawling, feuding, or falling in love). This attempt is never successful and can lead to either social renewal as illustrated in such comedies as *A Midsummer Night's*

Dream, where the young help integrate a new, more flexible social order by escaping the rigidity of the older generation, or to tragedy as the forces of flexibility, imagination, and transformation are destroyed by the rigidity of the older generation. Shakespeare was living through a period of rapid social, cultural, and technological change, and the interests and motivations of the younger generation were often in conflict with the more traditional values of the previous generation.

Act 1, Scene 2: This scene opens with Juliet's father, Capulet, engaged in a conversation with the County Paris, who wants to marry Juliet. We learn quickly that Juliet is the last of the Capulet's children; all the others have died, and that she is only 13 years old. We later discover that Juliet's mother is only 28, and it helps to understand the play if we keep the youth of these characters in mind. Juliet's father pushes the County Paris to wait two more years. We also find out that the Capulets have a party planned for that night. The scene shifts to Romeo and Benvolio, and their decision to crash the Capulet's party that evening. Benvolio hopes that Romeo will be able to compare the beauty of Rosaline with others at the party and so discover that other beautiful women exist and in this way cure Romeo of his "love." Romeo will go to the party, but he is sure that no person there will be able to compare to his Rosaline.

Act 1, Scene 3: The audience meets Juliet, her mother, and the Nurse in this scene as we learn that Juliet will turn fourteen in a little over two weeks. This scene is notable for the bawdy imagery and humor from the nurse, as well as our vision of a submissive Juliet who is willing to do what she needs to do to please her parents. Her mother introduces the idea of Juliet marrying the County Paris, and the imagery of flowers continues to be developed in this scene. The flower imagery associated with Juliet primarily suggests youth, romance, spring, and innocence. However, this image pattern of flowers is also associated with the goddess Persephone who spends half the year in the underworld. These flowers will be used during the scenes of Juliet's "death," and will suggest flowers blighted and destroyed before they have attained ripeness or maturity.

Another image pattern worth paying attention to here is that of reading and books (a pattern that will recur in the next scene when Juliet tells Romeo, "You kiss by th' book" (1.5.110). Juliet's mother says of the County Paris:

> This night you shall behold him at our feast;
>
> Read o'er the volume of young Paris' face,
>
> And find delight writ there with beauty's pen;
>
> Examine every married lineament,
>
> And see how one another lends content;
>
> And what obscur'd in this fair volume lies
>
> Find written in the margent of his eyes.
>
> This precious book of love, this unbound lover,
>
> To beautify him, only lacks a cover (1.3.80-88).

This imagery ties in with the earlier Petrarchan imagery associated with Romeo and gives the audience another "false" vision of love, of an idealized love that works according to rules and books and expectations—a concept of love that this play is designed to expose as false. Shakespeare does not believe that love is something that can be done "by the book." Real love is like the flashes of lightning or the explosions of gunpowder that Shakespeare develops as images related to the love of Romeo and Juliet.

Real love is far too powerful to be confined in the margins of a book. This contrast between false or artificial love and the reality of love is one of the primary themes of this play.

Another issue that appears over and over in Shakespeare is the theme of interpretation, and this theme is often presented in terms of "reading." One has to learn to "read" other people, to decode them, to be alert to the signs of social, cultural, and romantic codes. As a writer, Shakespeare was aware of the contrast between the artificial world of literature and the world that we actually inhabit with all of its passion, intensity, imperfection, and chaos. As much as we would like to confine things like love to a set of rules or expectations, there are always going to be unexpected consequences to love and unexpected aspects of personality. Who we love is not a matter of who our parents would like us to love, or even who we would like to love. This scene ends with a vision of Juliet as the dutiful daughter who responds to her mother's words about the County Paris with:

> I'll look to like, if looking liking move;
>
> But no more deep will I endart mine eye
>
> Than your consent gives strength to make [it] fly (1.3.97-99).

Juliet tells her mother that she will try to like the County if that's what her parents want, but she also reassures her mother that she will be sure not to like him more than her mother desires. Juliet wants to shape herself and her "love" to what her mother wants.

Act 1, Scene 4: This is one of the best known scenes of the play—the scene where we meet Romeo's friend Mercutio, a character whose very name tells the audience that he is a potentially transformative character, a character whose boundaries are fluid and changeable from one moment to the next. In this scene Mercutio, Romeo, Benvolio and others from the Montague house are on their way to crash the Capulet's party. Romeo hopes to see the object of his Petrarchan love, Rosaline, and Mercutio has a great time teasing Romeo about this idealized "love" at the beginning of the scene. This scene is another that is filled with bawdy humor although it is best known for Mercutio's Queen Mab speech and the introduction of the theme of dreams to the play. Dreams play an important role throughout the rest of the play.

Mercutio's long speech about dreams reveal him to be imaginative, flexible, and highly skilled with words. His character represents the possibility of change, but with his death in the third act, the possibility of transformation comes to an end. After his lengthy speech on Queen Mab, Romeo asks him to stop speaking, saying "Thou talk'st of nothing," (2.1.96), and Mercutio replies,

> True, I talk of dreams,
>
> Which are the children of an idle brain,
>
> Begot of nothing but vain fantasy,
>
> Which is as thin of substance as the air,
>
> And more inconstant than the wind…" (2.1.96-100).

Mercutio's long monologue on dreams makes a bit more sense if the audience realizes that the words "quean" and "mab" were both common terms for a promiscuous woman during Shakespeare's time. Mercutio is speaking of the power of desire throughout the monologue and Queen Mab represents that force. Romeo tells him he speaks of "nothing," and Mercutio agrees. "Nothing" was a slang word for a woman's sexual organs during the Renaissance.

Mercutio's monologue is one of the most fascinating in Shakespeare's writing, but it also illustrates how Shakespeare's writing works in many directions. Yes, it's a speech about dreams and the power of dreams and the imagination, but the speech is also about various kinds of desire and how these desires can deform rational thinking in an individual. The scene ends with Romeo having a sense of foreboding about the future and what it holds for him.

Act 1, Scene 5: In the last scene of Act 1, Romeo and Juliet encounter each other for the first time and fall in love at first sight. Important images that are developed in this scene include the hands that were introduced in the prologue, vision, honor, and love as a religion. For this masquerade Romeo is costumed as a palmer, a religious pilgrim, although Romeo's religion is the religion of romantic love. The first words spoken between Romeo and Juliet are in the form of a sonnet spoken in an exchange of lines between the two characters:

Rom. [*To Juliet.*] If I profane with my unworthiest hand

This holy shrine, the gentle sin is this,

My lips, two blushing pilgrims, ready stand

To smooth that rough touch with a tender kiss.

Jul. Good pilgrim, you do wrong your hand too much,

Which mannerly devotion shows in this:

For saints have hands that pilgrims' hands do touch,

And palm to palm is holy palmers' kiss.

Rom. Have not saints lips, and holy palmers too?

Jul. Ay, pilgrim, lips that they must use in pray'r.

Rom. O then, dear saint, let lips do what hands do,

They pray—grant thou, lest faith turn to despair.

Jul. Saints do not move, though grant for prayers' sake.

Rom. Then move not while my prayer's effect I take [*Kissing her*] (1.5.93-106).

The sonnet opens with religious imagery although this religion is the religion of love and is focused on this world and the pleasures of this world. Religious imagery becomes the imagery of physicality and of physical connection in this sonnet. Unlike the unattainable ideal of Rosalind or the Petrarchan ideal, this sonnet ends with a kiss, a consummation, with physical love and love made real. This kiss represents Romeo's rejection of the Petrarchan tradition. The imagery here is physical—of hands, palms, and lips. The imagery of hands was introduced in the sonnet that serves as the prologue to this play, and this imagery runs throughout the play. Shakespeare uses the imagery to emphasize the various ways hands can be used, and the hand imagery works as a kind of antithesis as the audience realizes that hands can fight, kill, and destroy as well as join, caress, and express love.

One thing to watch for throughout the remainder of the play is the way Shakespeare associates this intense romantic love with such imagery as lightning and gunpowder. Some lines from early in the play, *A Midsummer Night's Dream*, written about the same time as *Romeo and Juliet* and in many ways a comic treatment of the same issues and themes, illuminate Shakespeare's vision of "love at first sight." In *A Midsummer Night's Dream* we hear the lover Lysander say to his love, Hermia:

> Ay me! For aught that I could ever read,
>
> Could ever hear by tale or history,
>
> The course of true love never did run smooth;
>
> ...
>
> War, death, or sickness did lay siege to it,
>
> Making it momentary as a sound,
>
> Swift as a shadow, short as any dream,
>
> Brief as the lightning in the collied night
>
> ...
>
> So quick bright things come to confusion (1.1.132-149).

After their kiss, Romeo asks the Nurse who this stranger that he has seen for the first time is and discovers that she is a Capulet. Juliet also asks the Nurse who the young man is, and, when she discovers that he is a Montague, uses a series of antitheses, or conflicting statements, to describe her feelings:

> My only love sprung from my only hate!
>
> Too early seen unknown, and known too late!
>
> Prodigious birth of love it is to me
>
> That I must love a loathed enemy (1.5. 138-141).

This series of antithetical statements is built around the traditional Petrarchan theme of "the beloved enemy," and is in the traditional Petrarchan style; however, the love of Romeo and Juliet explodes the Petrarchan clichés of the "loathed enemy," and demonstrates the power of true love to overcome obstacles. A "prodigious birth," in the language of the time, means an unnatural birth.

Act 2, Prologue: The prologue to Act 2 is another sonnet. Here Shakespeare contrasts young love with old desire and brings in the themes of passion and extremes.

Act 2, Scene 1: This scene opens with Romeo avoiding his friends, Benvolio and Mercutio, although the majority of the scene is a bawdy discussion between Benvolio and Mercutio directed at what they still believe to be Romeo's infatuation with Rosaline. His friends call for Romeo, and Mercutio makes use of a bawdy "blazon" to try to get Romeo to join them. A blazon is another aspect of the Petrarchan tradition; it is a description of the physical beauty of the unattainable lover. Mercutio's bawdy blazon concerning Rosaline begins with the traditional Petrarchan description, but ends with a bawdy description of her:

> He heareth not, he stirreth not, he moveth not,
>
> The ape is dead, and I must conjure him.
>
> I conjure thee by Rosaline's bright eyes,
>
> By her high forehead and her scarlet lip,
>
> By her fine foot, straight leg, and quivering thigh,
>
> And the demesnes that there adjacent lie (2.1. 15-20).

The word "demesnes" is the modern word "domains," and refers to the parts of Rosalind near her "quivering thigh."

Mercutio continues in this bawdy vein, but when Romeo fails to appear, both Mercutio and Benvolio go home to sleep.

Act 2, Scene 2: This is the balcony scene, and one of the central scenes in the play. This scene is also the source of many of the best-known lines and images from *Romeo and Juliet*. In this scene Romeo steals into the garden of the Capulets and eavesdrops on Juliet as she stands on her balcony and muses on her new love for him. After he reveals himself to her, the two make vows to each other and plan to get married. This scene develops a number of imagery patterns, but among the most important are the continuing patterns of the hands and eyes. Romeo opens this scene by describing Juliet as the sun rising in the east and of her eyes as stars. He eavesdrops on Juliet as she speaks of their meeting that night before reveals himself to Juliet.

> As he listens to her, Romeo overhears Juliet say,
>
> O Romeo, Romeo, wherefore art thou Romeo?
>
> Deny Thy father and refuse thy name;
>
> Or, if thou wilt not, be but sworn my love,
>
> And I'll no longer be a Capulet.
>
> …
>
> 'Tis but thy name that is my enemy;
>
> Thou art thyself, though not a Montague.
>
> What's Montague? It is nor hand nor foot,
>
> Nor arm nor face, [nor any other part]
>
> Belonging to a man. O, be some other name!

> What's in a name? That which we call a rose
>
> By any other word would smell as sweet;
>
> So Romeo would, were he not Romeo called,
>
> Retain that dear perfection which he owes
>
> Without that title (2.2. 33-47).

When Juliet uses the word, "wherefore," here, it means "why," not "where." In other words Juliet is asking why Romeo has to be a son of her family's enemy "clan," the Montagues. If he had been a member of another family there would not have been such a barrier between them.

Juliet is also trying to pierce the veil of language here and understand the reality that lies underneath such things as names, labels, and words. For Juliet "reality" is something that goes far beyond words. Words can hint at deeper truths, but words are unable to capture that underlying reality of being and identity.

Shakespeare develops imagery of the sun and moon throughout this scene as well, although he inverts the normal ways in which sun and moon imagery are used. The moon is traditionally associated with women and the sun with men, but in this scene Romeo is associated with the moon and Juliet with the sun. Writers of Shakespeare's time, and earlier, traditionally associated the moon, and women, with inconstancy and change while the sun was associated with men as well as constancy and loyalty. When Romeo uses the moon to swear to the strength of his love for Juliet, she corrects him and says,

> O, swear not by the moon, th' inconstant moon,
>
> That monthly changes in her [circled] orb,

Lest that thy love prove likewise variable (2.2.109-111).

Juliet wants to know that she can depend upon Romeo and that his love for will not change. Although she doesn't know about Rosaline, the audience is very aware of Romeo's potential for "inconstancy" or changing the woman he is "in love" with. Romeo asks what he should swear by, and she tells him not to swear at all or to swear by himself and his faithfulness to her.

Juliet is a realist, though, and she understands the potential problems that could develop from loving Romeo. She tells him,

> Although I joy in thee,
>
> I have no joy of this contract to-night,
>
> It is too rash, too unadvis'd, too sudden,
>
> Too like the lightning, which doth cease to be
>
> Ere one can say it lightens. Sweet, good night!
>
> This bud of love, by summer's ripening breath,
>
> May prove a beauteous flow'r when next we meet (2.2. 116-120).

This speech reinforces the theme of time and the potential of hasty actions ending in disaster. Juliet is concerned that the two young people are acting too quickly and on their on, without advice from more experienced counselors. The image of the lightning that briefly flashes, then disappears, is an image that she fears. Will there be enough light from their love to allow the two lovers to escape the difficulties of their families?

Juliet follows these questions with the lines that Harold Bloom refers to as the greatest epiphany of romantic love in western literature when Juliet speaks of her love for Romeo:

> My bounty is as boundless as the sea,
>
> My love as deep; the more I give to thee,
>
> The more I have, for both are infinite (2.2.133-135).

Juliet's beautiful lines speak to one of the central paradoxes about love, about giving—the more love one gives, the more love one has to give. This brilliant speech challenges the idea of scarcity and replaces it with one of abundance and fulfillment.

This crucial scene includes a number of other image patterns that are important to *Romeo and Juliet* such as light and dark, gardens, falcons and falconry, birds, and music.

Act 2, Scene 3: In this scene we meet Romeo's friend and advisor, Friar Lawrence. Both Friar Lawrence and the Nurse serve as older, more experienced, advisors to the young lovers. This scene opens with the Friar gathering medicinal herbs. As he gathers these herbs, he reflects on the various uses of plants and how each plant has its uses. The world of plants is symbolic of both God's order and of the disorder that rules the physical world humans inhabit. Like the plants in God's garden each human individual has a use, a purpose, a role to fulfill:

> O, mickle is the powerful grace that lies
>
> In plants, herbs, stones, and their true qualities;
>
> For nought so vile that on the earth doth live
>
> But to the earth some special good doth give;

Nor aught so good but, strain'd from that fair use,

Revolts from true birth, stumbling on abuse.

Virtue itself turns vice, being misapplied,

And vice sometime by action dignified.

Within the infant rind of this weak flower

Poison hath residence and medicine power;

For this, being smelt, with that part cheers each part,

Being tasted, stays all senses with the heart.

Two such opposed kings encamp them still

In man as well as herbs, grace and rude will;

And where the worser is predominant,

Full soon the canker death eats up that plant (2.3. 15-30).

The word "mickle" means "great," and Friar Lawrence is addressing both the great power for good or evil that plants and other elements of the natural world contain. He then explicitly links these antithetical qualities with humans, underscoring the way Shakespeare uses this imagery has to connect humans with the rest of the natural world. Like the rest of the world, humans have opposing forces within them—a force that pulls us toward goodness and a force that pulls us toward ego and the assertion of our wills over others and the world. If the negative side predominates in an individual, that person will, like a plant, be destroyed by a "canker" or cancer that will eat the person from within. Practically all of Friar Lawrence's lines rhyme, a poetic device that Shakespeare uses to let the audience know that the Friar is at one with the order of nature, that he lives a harmonious life.

Romeo appears and, after a moment of confusion on Friar Lawrence's part when he thinks Romeo is talking about Rosalind, Friar Lawrence warns Romeo about "doting" or infatuation and the problems that can come from doting. Earlier both Romeo and Juliet have talked about eyes in relationship to love. Friar Lawrence wants to make sure that Romeo, having succumbed to love at first "sight," is not simply infatuated by Juliet's beauty—that he loves with more than his eyes:

Holy Saint Francis, what a change is here!

Is Rosaline, that thou didst love so dear,

So soon forsaken? Young men's love then lies

Not truly in their hearts but in their eyes (2.3. 65-68).

Friar Lawrence eventually agrees to help Romeo in his quest for Juliet since he hopes that a marriage between the two families will bring an end to the ancient feud between the Montagues and Capulets. Romeo wants to be married immediately, and the Friar warns Romeo about the dangers of haste and of moving too quickly in the last line of the scene: "Wisely and slow, they stumble that run fast" (2.3. 94).

Act 2, Scene 4: This is one of the great comic scenes in the play. It opens with Mercutio and Benvolio wondering where Romeo is, and, not knowing about Juliet, speaking, in bawdy terms, of his infatuation with Rosaline. Mercutio also discusses Tybalt and his willingness to fight, describing his attraction to fighting with imagery of music and dance: "He fights as you sing prick-song, keeps time, distance, and proportion; he rests his minim rests, one, two, and the third in your bosom: the very butcher of a silk button, a duelist, a duelist" (2.4. 20-24). "Prick-song" means printed music, and a minim is a short musical rest. This description of Tybalt as a fighter makes clear that he knows all the "moves" in a duel, and that he is able to use them well. After Romeo joins his two friends, Mercutio once more turns to bawdy humor at Romeo's expense, making fun of him and his supposed love for Rosaline. During a brief speech, Mercutio refers to Romeo's hyperbolic "love" for Rosaline in words that call up the Petrarchan tradition, but also make reference to many of the best-known women from the ancient world:

> Now is he for the numbers that Petrarch flowed in. Laura to his lady was a kitchen wench (marry, she had a better love to berhyme her), Dido a dowdy, Cleopatra a gipsy, Helen and Hero hildings and harlots, Thisby a grey eye or so, but not to the purpose (2.4. 38-43).

Petrarch is the patron saint of the sonnet sequence that celebrates the beauty of the woman the writer loves but cannot have. Dido, Cleopatra, Helen, Hero, and Thisby all feature as beautiful women in classical literature. The word "hilding" in this speech means "good-for-nothing."

The humor continues with the appearance of the Nurse who has come from Juliet with a message for Romeo. Mercutio makes the Nurse the butt of several bawdy jokes. Eventually Romeo is able to have a private conference with the Nurse and tells her that Friar Lawrence will perform a marriage for the two lovers that afternoon. The Nurse leaves to tell Juliet of the plans.

Act 2, Scene 5: This scene opens with Juliet in an impatient state as she waits for the Nurse to return and inform her of the results of the meeting with Romeo. Once more Shakespeare plays with the themes of time and hasty actions. Juliet wants to know the results of the meeting with Romeo immediately, but the Nurse has fun at the expense of Juliet by delaying in telling Juliet what the plan will be. The scene ends with the Nurse telling Juliet to go to Friar Lawrence that afternoon, and that he will perform the marriage. The Nurse plans to get a ladder that Romeo can use to sneak into Juliet's room that night, after the wedding has been performed.

Act 2, Scene 6 This scene shows Romeo and Juliet being married, but also includes words of warning about haste and passion—words that will come back to haunt the audience as the play shifts from a comic vision to a tragic vision. The scene opens with Friar Lawrence asking the heavens to bless this "holy act." Romeo's response is to speak of the joy he has seeing Juliet and to ask the Friar to "close our hands with holy words" (6). The imagery of the hands joining together uses the old language of taking a person's hand in marriage but also the joining of two lives and two families in to a whole. Romeo speaks with such impatience, however, that Friar Lawrence warns him:

> These violent delights have violent ends,
>
> And in their triumph die, like fire and power,
>
> Which as they kiss consume. The sweetest honey
>
> Is loathsome in his own deliciousness,
>
> And in the taste confounds the appetite.
>
> Therefore love moderately: long love doth so;
>
> Too swift arrives as tardy as too slow (2.6. 9-15).

The Friar's imagery contrasts violence and intensity with moderation. Shakespeare uses the imagery of gunpowder

The Make It Fun Guide to Romeo and Juliet

and fire again in this speech to reinforce the explosive nature of an intense love that consumes itself in the act of being joined. Friar Lawrence also warns Romeo that if anything is taken to excess, it will be unpleasing and emphasizes the importance of taking thinks slowly. Juliet enters, and the scene ends with the exit of the three so that the Friar can perform the marriage.

Act 3, Scene 1: Act 3 shifts the play toward its tragic movement when Benvolio and Mercutio encounter Tybalt and the Capulets. Romeo attempts to stop the duel between Mercutio and Tybalt and unwittingly brings about Mercutio's death. Mercutio, for all his flaws, represents the possibility of transformation and change in the play, and after his death the play moves inexorably toward the tragic ending. After the death of Mercutio, Romeo and Tybalt duel and Tybalt, now Romeo's unwitting kinsman, is slain. Tybalt's death results in Romeo's banishment from Verona.

This scene builds upon a conflict between the honor code with its rigid rules for vengeance and the possibility for transformation offered by love or by compassion and the willingness to overlook mistakes and insults. By succumbing to the demands of the honor code, Romeo becomes implicated in the tragic conclusion of the play. Another topic this scene raises is the construction of maleness, and the question of what it means to be a male. To this point in the play the audience has seen Romeo as the Petrarchan lover or the actual lover, but here he briefly succumbs to the demands of the "honor" code, of being a "man" in the medieval sense of chivalry, swordsmanship, and dueling. After the death of Mercutio, Romeo states:

O sweet Juliet,

Thy beauty hath made me effeminate

And in my temper soft'ned valor's steel (3.1.113-115).

In other words, his love for Juliet has "unmanned" him, and his need to avenge his friend becomes more important than his love. By accepting the ideas of maleness represented by the honor code, Romeo falls away from an authentic self into one that fits the demands of society—demands of rigidity rather than transformation. An honor code built around revenge represents inflexibility and the inability to move forward; this is precisely the opposite of the life promised by love and transformation. Romeo falls into the formalized roles of the past and of living a role imposed on him by external pressures rather than being his authentic self, and so the tragic action of the play accelerates. Romeo moves from love to revenge and invokes the elemental imagery of fire to express his desire for revenge: "Away to heaven, respective lenity,/And fire-[ey'd] fury be my conduct now" (3.1.123-124).

The tragic action begins almost as a joke. Benvolio is trying to persuade Mercutio to leave a public area so that they won't run into Tybalt and the Capulets, but Mercutio refuses and the two discuss which is the readiest to quarrel. Tybalt enters and speaks to Mercutio, saying that he "consortest" with Romeo. To "consort" with is to spend time together, but this word also refers to a musical consort or group or even concert. The word also refers to a sexual connection. Mercutio willingly misinterprets Tybalt's word and using the imagery of music and dance pulls his sword, saying,

> Consort! What, dost, thou make us minstrels? And thou make minstrels of us,
> look to hear nothing but discords. Here's my fiddlestick, here's that shall make
> you dance.'Zounds consort! (3.1. 45-49).

The word "zounds" here is a contraction for "God's wounds," an expression that, in its full form, was considered blasphemous. A modern example would be the word "darn" substituting for "damn."

Romeo enters and Tybalt tells Mercutio that it is Romeo he seeks, and so he will not fight Mercutio. Tybalt attempts to engage Romeo in a quarrel, telling him that Romeo has insulted Tybalt and his family. Romeo refuses to be drawn into the quarrel and Mercutio, the cynic who ridicules both love and the honor code, allows himself to be drawn into the quarrel, saying of Romeo's refusal to fight, "O calm, dishonorable, vile submission!" (3.1. 73) and drawing his sword.

Romeo attempts to intervene and steps between Tybalt and Mercutio and during this attempt at intervention, Tybalt stabs Mercutio. Mercutio says,

> I am hurt.
>
> A plague a' both houses! I am sped.
>
> Is he gone and hath nothing? (3.1.90-92).

Even as he dies Mercutio jokes and makes use of puns. Romeo tells Mercutio to have courage and that the hurt can't be too severe, and Mercutio responds:

No, 'tis not so deep as a well, nor so wide as a church door, but 'tis enough, 'twill
serve. Ask for me to-morrow, and you shall find me a grave man. I am pepper'd, I
warrant for this world. A plague a' both your houses! 'Zounds, a dog, a rat, a
mouse, a cat, to scratch a man to death! A braggart, a rogue, a villain, that fights
by the book of arithmetic! Why the dev'l came you between us? I was hurt under
you're arm" (3.1. 96-103).

Mercutio is even able to make puns about his death as he says he will be a "grave," or serious, man the next day, but also that he is a man destined for the grave. He realizes that he has been killed as a result of the enmities generated by the feud, but he is also angry that he has been killed by Tybalt, a man he considers to be less skilled at fencing than himself. He reduces Tybalt to animal status, but is also angry because he "fights by the book," another instance of book imagery being used to describe a person who has learned to do something through instruction books and rules rather than through experience. Ultimately, however, he blames Romeo for stepping between them and trying to stop the duel. This action can serve as almost a summary statement for the entire play. Romeo, Juliet, and Friar Lawrence all try to recreate this rigid world of feuds and honor, but their attempts end only in destruction.

Romeo's response to Mercutio's death is to seek revenge. Romeo falls into the role society expects of him and in doing so loses the ability to define himself. The possibilities for change and forgiveness that he has been moving toward evaporate when says:

Away to heaven, respective lenity,

> And fire-[ey'd] fury be my conduct now!
>
> Now, Tybalt, take the "villain" back again
>
> That late thou gavest me, for Mercutio's soul
>
> Is but a little way above our heads,
>
> Staying for thine to keep him company (3.1. 123-128).

Romeo kills Tybalt in the fight that follows, and after killing Tybalt states, "O, I am fortune's fool!" (3.1. 136). Romeo, by allowing himself to be defined by the expectations of society and its reliance on the honor code and traditional gender roles that define a man as someone who seeks revenge and relies on violence now loses control over his destiny and his future. By fulfilling these expectations, he puts himself in the hands of society and the Prince and loses his individual freedom.

This scene ends with the Prince banishing Romeo from Verona. Not only does this show the continuing futile attempt of the prince to impose order on disorder through his decrees and rigidity, but it also raises one of Shakespeare's omnipresent themes—the relationship of justice to mercy. The rigidity of the Prince and his attempt to create order is signaled in the way the prince addresses this theme in the last two lines of this scene:

> Bear hence this body and attend our will;
>
> Mercy but murders, pardoning those that kill (3.1.196-197).

The Prince is, in the Elizabethan worldview, the representative of God and God's order in the earthly world. This disorderly world resists order, however, and the Prince is not successful. He does show mercy in banishing Romeo rather than executing him, but he also realizes the limits of mercy and that mercy will not satisfy the demands of the code of honor and revenge.

Act 3, Scene 2: This scene opens with Juliet anxiously awaiting the arrival of Romeo and the consummation of their marriage. Juliet's opening speech in this scene is a kind of hymn in praise of night and the delights that night will bring, but Juliet's joyful anticipation of the coming night is brought to a swift conclusion when the Nurse enters with news of Tybalt's death at Romeo's hand. Juliet is at first confused by the Nurse and Juliet thinks that Romeo is dead. When she learns that Romeo has slain Tybalt, her language takes on the inauthenticity of the Petrarchan tradition we earlier saw Romeo using in his imagined "relationship" with Rosaline. Juliet speaks in the antitheses and paradoxes that characterize this tradition with such lines as "fiend angelical/Dove-feather's raven! Wolvish ravening lamb" (3.2.75-76). These are images that are similar to Romeo's earlier images of "brawling love" or "heavy lightness." Juliet says that Romeo is an angel but also a fiend or a lamb that slaughters in the same way a wolf does. These impossible images reveal the deep conflicts Juliet feels about her love for Romeo as well as her love for her cousin, Tybalt.

Juliet also falls back into using the imagery of books as her mother did when praising the County Paris, or as Mercutio did in describing Tybalt as a swordsman. Juliet uses the book imagery to personify the old cliché that one can't "judge a book by its cover" when she asks,

> Was ever book containing such vile matter
>
> So fairly bound? O that deceit should dwell
>
> In such a gorgeous palace! (3.2. 83-85).

Juliet is wondering how something so beautiful on the outside as Romeo could be so bad on the inside. Juliet is grieving for her dead cousin, but as soon as the nurse speaks poorly of Romeo, Juliet pulls back and begins to defend her husband. Her true self reappears as she says, in response to the Nurse's question, "Will you speak well of him that kill'd your cousin?" (3.2. 96).

    Shall I speak ill of him that is my husband?

    Ah, poor my lord, what tongue shall smooth thy name,

    When I, thy three-hours wife, have mangled it? …

    My husband lives that Tybalt would have slain,

    And Tybalt's dead that would have slain my husband.

    All this is comfort, wherefore weep I then? (3.2.97-108).

    Just as in the balcony scene, Juliet addresses the issue of names or labels and recognizes that names are frequently unable to capture the reality expressed by the name. This scene ends with Juliet speaking to the rope ladder that was supposed to be Romeo's entrance to her balcony that night:

    Take up those cords. Poor ropes, you are beguil'd,

    Both you and I, for Romeo is exil'd

    He made you for a highway to my bed,

    But I, a maid, die maiden-widowed.

    Come, cords, come, nurse, I'll to my wedding-bed

And death, not Romeo, take my maidenhead!

These lines foreshadow Juliet's coming "death" from the cordial that the Friar will give her as well as her eventual death from love, as Shakespeare continues to explore the relationship of love and death that is so powerful throughout this play.

The Nurse ends the scene by telling Juliet that she knows where Romeo is and will make sure he comes to Juliet that night. Juliet tells her to find Romeo and bring him to "take his last farewell."

Act 3, Scene 3: This scene opens with Romeo in Friar Lawrence's cell; Romeo is groaning about his fate, and Friar Lawrence is berating him for not realizing his blessings. Key elements of this scene explore the nature of maleness and whether or not Romeo is living up the expectations of how a man should behave. To the Friar's encouraging statement that he is only banished and not sentenced to death, Romeo replies with a central image of the microcosm/macrocosm. The Friar tells Romeo to be encouraged "for the world is broad and wide" (3.3.16) and Romeo replies, "There is not world without Verona walls,/But purgatory, torture, hell itself (3.3.17-18). "Microcosm" means "small world" and occurs in literature or art when something small is used to represent the larger world. In medieval and renaissance times the world was often represented as a "ship of fools." An example from our own time is the *Starship Enterprise* in the science fiction series and films, *StarTrek*. Romeo sees no world except that of Verona. The Friar tells Romeo that he is being ungrateful and doesn't recognize the mercy (as opposed to justice) that he is receiving here. Friar Lawrence attempts to give him a philosophical approach to events, which Romeo rejects. Romeo then falls to the ground.

The Nurse enters and she and the Friar discuss the piteous state of the two lovers as well as Romeo's failure to act like a man and "stand up." The nurse makes the parallel between Romeo, male, and Juliet, female, explicit when she speaks of his self-indulgent "grief" in response to Friar Lawrence's statement that Romeo is "There on the ground, with his own tears made drunk" (3.3.83):

> O, he is even in my mistress' case,
>
> Just in her case, O woeful sympathy!
>
> Piteous predicament! Even so lies she,
>
> Blubb'ring and weeping, weeping and blubb'ring
>
> Stand up, stand up, stand, and you be a man.
>
> For Juliet's sake, for her sake, rise and stand;
>
> Why should you fall into so deep an O? (3.3.84-90).

Romeo does rise at these words but then attempts to stab himself. At this point Friar Lawrence accuses him of being not only womanly but bestial:

> Hold thy desperate hand!
>
> Art thou a man? Thy form cries out thou art;
>
> Thy tears are womanish, thy wild acts [denote]
>
> The unreasonable fury of a beast
>
> Unseemly woman in a seeming man,
>
> And ill-seeming beast in seeming both,
>
> Thou has amaz'd me! (3.3.108-114).

The Friar then tells Romeo what a man should be, once more using the image of gunpowder, and lists the many ways in which Romeo has been blessed rather than cursed. Friar Lawrence closes this scene by encouraging Romeo to go to Juliet's chamber to consummate the marriage before his departure for Mantua.

Act 3, Scene 4: This scene sets up a new obstacle for Juliet and her love for Romeo. Her father and County Paris set the day that she will be married to the County. The scene opens with her father finalizing plans for Juliet's marriage with the County Paris. Her father still views Juliet as a child, but, even more importantly, as his possession to dispose of as he wishes:

> Sir Paris, I will make a desperate tender
>
> Of my child's love. I think she will [be] rul'd
>
> In all respects by me; nay more, I doubt it not (3.4.12-14).

He and Paris plan for the wedding to take place in three days; today is Monday and the marriage will take place on Thursday.

Act 3, Scene 5: This scene presents the culmination of the love of Romeo and Juliet as well as their last meeting while still alive. The scene opens with Romeo preparing to depart after the one night they spend in each other's arms, the night in which they consummate their marriage. Juliet does not want Romeo to leave and claims that the bird which awakened him is the nightingale, a bird of the night, and not the lark, a bird of the early morning. This scene continues to develop the imagery of light and dark and of torches that penetrate the night. Romeo says he will stay and welcome death if Juliet wills it. At this point she realizes the danger and tells him to go:

> Hie hence, be gone, away!
>
> It is the lark that sings so out of tune,
>
> Straining harsh discords and unpleasing sharps.
>
> Some say the lark makes sweet division;
>
> This doth not so, for she divideth us (3.5.26-30).

This image of the lark's sweet song as discordant underscores how unnatural it is for these lovers to be divided rather than united in their love, and Romeo's next line furthers that sense of unnaturalness through the rhetorical figure of paradox, "More light and light, more dark and dark our woes" (3.5.36).

The Nurse enters with news that Juliet's mother is coming to see her, and Romeo departs for Mantua and his banishment. When her mother enters Juliet's chamber, she misreads Juliet's grief and thinks Juliet is distraught over Tybalt's death. She promises to see to it that Romeo will be poisoned in Mantua. Juliet encourages her mother in this misreading and in the process says that she too wishes to see Romeo poisoned and dead. This, ironically, foreshadows Romeo's actual death in Act 5.

Juliet's mother also brings news of the upcoming marriage to Paris, and, faced with this dilemma, Juliet stands up for herself and refuses the marriage. After Juliet's father is informed of her refusal to marry Paris, he and Juliet argue. Both her mother and father eventually say they would rather she were dead than disobedient. Her mother states, "I would the fool were married to her grave!" (3.5.140), and her father threatens both violence and banishment from the family:

> Hang thee, young baggage! Disobedient wretch!

> I tell thee what: get thee to church a'Thursday,
>
> Or never after look me in the face.
>
> Speak not, reply not, do not answer me!
>
> My fingers itch. Wife, we scarce thought us blest
>
> That God had lent us but this only child,
>
> But now I see this one is one too much,
>
> And that we have in having her.
>
> ...
>
> And you be mine, I'll give you to my friend;
>
> And you be not, hang, beg, starve, die in the streets,
>
> For by my soul, I'll ne'er acknowledge thee,
>
> Nor what is mine shall never do thee good (3.5.160-194).

Once more an authority figure tries to force "disorder" into order. Just as with the Prince's decree that there will be no more brawling in the city, this attempt to force a raging river into a narrow channel will end in disaster. This theme surfaces over and over in Shakespeare, but nowhere so tellingly as in *Romeo and Juliet*. The energies of the world, of such fundamental forces as love, are beyond human attempts to control them and eventually destroy those who futilely try to force dominion where none is to be had.

After the exit of her father and mother, Juliet seeks counsel from her nurse who recommends that she obey her father since Romeo has been banished. The Nurse tells Juliet to marry the County Paris. The nurse, for all her attractiveness as a comic character, here reveals herself to be a bad or false counselor to Juliet. Juliet adopts a staged character, acts a part, and tells the Nurse to inform her father that she has gone to see Friar Lawrence to make confession, and that she will do what her father desires.

However, as soon as the Nurse has departed and Juliet is alone, she reveals her true purposes and her insights into the nature of the Nurse:

Ancient damnation! O most wicked fiend!

Is it more sin to wish me thus forsworn,

Or to dispraise my lord with that same tongue

Which she hath prais'd him with above compare

So many thousand times? Go, counsellor,

Thou and my bosom henceforth shall be twain.

I'll to the friar to know his remedy;

If all else fail, myself have power to die (3.5.235-242).

For all those who claim that the Nurse is their favorite character after a reading or viewing of *Romeo and Juliet*, it's worth paying attention to Juliet's words here. This "comic" counselor has become "ancient damnation" and a "wicked fiend." She is clearly associated with demonic energies of chaos and disorder through Juliet's words. Over the course of this play, Juliet is consistently the character with the most insight and, and her words shed a revealing light on the Nurse and her role in the play. The Nurse is really little more than a panderer, a pimp, willing to serve any master—as long as that master will reward her.

Act 4, Scene 1: This scene opens with a brief discussion between the County Paris and Friar Lawrence about the upcoming wedding of Juliet and the County. The Friar is disquieted by the news of this upcoming wedding. Juliet enters and responds to the County Paris' greeting and comment about the wedding with a reference to the unchangeable nature of fate, "What must be shall be" (4.1.21) which is followed by the Friar's comment, "That's a certain text" (4.1.22). This increasing emphasis on fate and our lack of freedom to do as we will contributes to the growing sense of tragic inevitability that marks the second half of this play.

After the departure of Paris, the Friar and Juliet try to decide what to do about the proposed marriage. This scene continues the imagery of hands and Juliet threatens to commit suicide with a knife, saying:

> And with this knife I'll help it presently.
>
> God join'd my heart and Romeo's, thou our hands,
>
> And ere this hand, by thee to Romeo's seal'd,
>
> Shall be the label to another deed,
>
> Or my true heart with treacherous revolt
>
> Turn to another, this shall slay them both (4.1. 54-59).

Juliet uses the images of joined hands on earth as an emblem, or symbol, of the eternal joining of their hearts by God. Juliet also uses imagery of labels or names and their relationship to the meanings they stand for here. She refuses to allow a false label to be placed on her, one that would deny her love for Romeo.

Juliet says she would rather hide in a charnel house (a tomb) than marry Paris and betray Romeo, once again foreshadowing her imminent death. Friar Lawrence grasps this suggestion by Juliet, and proposes a plan to simulate, or fake, her death, so that she can escape the planned marriage to Paris and be reunited with Romeo. The Friar unfolds his plan and bids Juliet go home, promise to marry Paris, and be merry. The Friar's plan is for Juliet to drink a potion that will put her in a death-like state for 42 hours, after which she will awaken and be joined with Romeo. The Friar plans to send a letter to Romeo to let him know of the plan. Friar Lawrence hopes to bring order to this disordered affair. This will not be the case as the remainder of the play unfolds, but the audience does get the outlines of a possible solution to the difficulties faced by the lovers.

Act 4, Scene 2: In this short scene, Juliet apologizes to her father for her disobedience and promises to follow his directives and wed the County the next day. Juliet is lying to her father in order to make sure that she can put Friar Lawrence's plan into action and thus escape the planned marriage with Paris.

Act 4, Scene 3: This scene opens with Juliet saying good night to her Mother and the Nurse, and then, alone, she thinks of what lies before her:

Farewell! God knows when we shall meet again.

I have a faint cold fear thrills through my veins,

That almost freezes up the heat of life.

I'll call them back again to comfort me.

Nurse!—What should she do here?

My dismal scene I needs must act alone.

This scene shows that Juliet is aware that she is playing a part in a larger drama. She thinks of herself as an actress performing a role when she says, "My dismal scene I needs must act alone" (4.3.19). As Juliet prepares to drink the Friar's potion, she reviews the horrors that lie before her in the tomb, but the strength of her love drives her to drink, and the scene ends with her falling, apparently dead, on her bed.

Act 4, Scene 4: This short scene begins with Juliet's parents preparing for the wedding and ends with the Nurse being sent to awaken Juliet and to help her get ready for the wedding.

Act 4, Scene 5: This scene opens with the Nurse attempting to awaken Juliet only to discover that she is "dead." The wedding mirth quickly turns to grief, and Juliet's father repeatedly uses images of flowers to speak of her sudden death in such passages as, "Death lies on her like an untimely frost/Upon the sweetest flower of all the field" (4.5.28-29). Juliet was his only living child. Her father says to Paris:

> O son, the night before thy wedding-day
>
> Hath Death lain with thy wife. There she lies,
>
> Flower as she was, deflowered by him.
>
> Death is my son-in-law, Death is my heir,
>
> My daughter he hath wedded (4.5. 35-39).

These lines use flower imagery and establish a connection with Persephone, the daughter of Ceres who was kidnapped by Pluto, the ruler of the underworld and taken to Hades. In imagery that recalls both the opening scene and the joking just before the brawl as well as the consummated wedding between Romeo and Juliet, her father refers to her virginity or maidenhead being taken by Death and not a living person (her father certainly doesn't know about Romeo's visit to her bedroom). After Capulet's words, the other three who are present in the room, Lady Capulet, the Nurse, and the County Paris, each address Juliet's body and Death.

Friar Lawrence counsels them to have peace since Juliet is now better off. Her father finally speaks of how her "death" has turned everything upside down:

> All things that we ordained festival,
>
> Turn from their office to black funeral:
>
> Our instruments to melancholy bells,
>
> Our weeding cheer to a sad burial feast;
>
> Our solemn hymns to sullen dirges change;
>
> Our bridal flowers serve for a buried corse;
>
> And all things change them to the contrary (4.5. 84-90).

These images of joy and mirth turned to sadness and despair are appropriate for a play in which the joys of young love have been turned upside down and made the source of a tragedy. This scene ends with a comic interaction between the Nurse's servant, Peter, and the musicians who had been hired to play at the wedding. This final part of the scene is filled with puns and a discussion of music and how it affects our moods. This conclusion to the scene also provides comic relief for the audience.

Act 5, Scene 1: This scene opens with Romeo, in Mantua, thinking about the dreams he had the night before, and believing that these dreams foreshadow the arrival of joyful news. This dream speaks to the truth of the situation for Juliet only appears to be dead, and she will soon be "resurrected" to join him. Unfortunately, he doesn't know to trust his dream, which reveals the truth, over apparent reality which, in this case, hides the truth. Romeo's servant, Balthasar, arrives with news of Juliet's "death." Romeo doesn't trust his own dreams and intuitive knowledge in the face of this eye-witness report from Balthasar. This does provide an excellent illustration of the concept of dramatic irony since the audience knows that Juliet is actually alive while Romeo believes she is dead and acts on that belief. Dramatic irony takes place when the audience possesses information that the actors don't have and can be used, as in this instance, to create powerful suspense and tension in the audience. This is also an example of the theme of haste. Romeo is going to act in haste on Balthasar's information, and he is going to act without any additional confirmation of Juliet's death from a long-standing advisor such as Friar Lawrence.

Romeo's response to the news of Juliet's death illustrates the growth of his character. His language as he responds to Balthasar reflects that growth. At the beginning of the play Romeo spoke in the artificial language of Petrarchanism. Here his language is direct, simple, and straightforward:

Is it [e'en] so? Then I [defy] you stars!

Thou knowest my lodging, get me ink and paper,

And hire post-horses; I will hence to-night (5.1.24-26).

Romeo then speaks to himself and says that he will "lie" with Juliet tonight. He seeks out an apothecary (pharmacist), purchases poison from the reluctant apothecary, and ends the scene by addressing the poison as a cordial, or health-giving medicine, not a poison, and restating his intention to visit Juliet's grave and there poison himself. This apothecary, who provides death, is a doubling of Friar Lawrence, a doubling which echoes the Friar's earlier speech about the qualities of plants and how what is good can also be evil. Friar Lawrence has also provided a "poison" that will simulate death in order to create life, but this apothecary provides a poison that will destroy life. The words Romeo speaks to end this scene reinforce this sense of doubleness:

> Come, cordial and not poison, go with me
>
> To Juliet's grave, for there must I use thee (5.1. 85-86).

Romeo wants to die and be with Juliet in death, and so this poison will become a cordial, or healthy drink to him which allows him to join Juliet in what he thinks is her death.

Act 5, Scene 2: This brief scene between Friar Lawrence and Friar John informs the audience that Romeo has not received the letter Friar Lawrence sent since Friar John was quarantined due to fear of plague in the city. Sine he was quarantined, Friar John was unable to deliver the letter. As all things seem to line up against Romeo and Juliet, it does indeed seem that the fates or their crossed starts will not allow a happy ending for these young lovers.

Act 5, Scene 3: This final scene opens with the County Paris visiting Juliet's tomb and continues the imagery of flowers that is so central to this play. Paris speaks to the tomb with the words, "Sweet flower, with flowers thy bridal bed I strew/O woe, thy canopy is dust and stones!" (5.3. 12-13). As Paris addresses the tomb of Juliet, his servant warns him that someone is approaching. Paris retires and a distraught Romeo enters. Once more Romeo envisions himself as a beast, and, after giving Balthasar a letter to deliver warns Balthasar not to interrupt him as he plans to break open the tomb and to join Juliet inside:

> The time and my intents are savage wild,
>
> More fierce and more inexorable far
>
> Than empty tigers or the roaring sea (5.3.37-39).

Balthasar exits and Romeo attacks the door of the tomb. Paris interrupts Romeo, and even though Romeo warns Paris and says he doesn't want to hurt him, the two fight, and Romeo kills Paris; Romeo doesn't know who he is fighting until after he has killed him. Romeo enters the tomb and addresses Juliet in words that recall the myth of Persephone once more:

> Ah, dear Juliet,
>
> Why art thou yet so fair? Shall I believe
>
> That unsubstantial Death is amorous,
>
> And that the lean abhorred monster keeps
>
> Thee here in dark to be his paramour? (5.3. 101-105).

Romeo then drinks the poison he has brought with him. Romeo's last utterance is, "Thus with a kiss I die" (5.3.120). This final utterance clearly reminds the audience that he is dying for love.

Friar Lawrence now enters the tomb so that he can be there for Juliet when she awakens, and discovers the bodies of both Paris and Romeo. Juliet awakens, and Friar

Lawrence attempts to persuade her to leave the tomb. He brings up the concept of fate to Juliet as he tells her:

> A greater power than we can contradict
>
> Hath thwarted our intents. Come, come away.
>
> Thy husband in thy bosom there lies dead;
>
> And Paris too. Come, I'll dispose of thee
>
> Among a sisterhood of holy nuns (5.3. 154-159).

Friar Lawrence hears the calls of the approaching watch, and he flees the tomb, demonstrating his ultimate cowardice, and leaving Juliet alone in the tomb with the body of Romeo. Juliet looks at Romeo's body, and says, "Poison, I see, hath been his timeless end" (5.3.162) and tries to drink from the same vial only to realize that all the poison is gone. She then uses Romeo's dagger to stab herself.

The watch appears and the bodies of Romeo and Juliet are discovered. The families of the Capulets and the Montagues as well as the Prince arrive at the tomb, and Friar Lawrence explains the sequence of events and his failed plan to reunite the lovers. The Prince now addresses the families, asking,

> Where be these enemies? Capulet! Montague!
>
> See what a scourge is laid upon your hate,
>
> That heaven finds means to kill your joys with love,
>
> And I for winking at your discords too
>
> Have lost a brace of kinsmen. All are punish'd (5.3.291-295).

Capulet and Montague now take each other's hands and promise to erect statues of pure gold of Juliet and Romeo and to end the enmity between their families. The Prince concludes the play with this speech:

> A glooming peace this morning with it brings,
>
> The sun, for sorrow, will not show his head.
>
> Go hence to have more talk of these sad things;
>
> Some shall be pardon'd, and some punished:
>
> For never was a story of more woe
>
> Than this of Juliet and her Romeo (5.3.305-310).

Themes

When reading this play, keep in mind that Shakespeare is not following the typical pattern for classical tragedy which involves high born characters who suffer from a tragic character flaw. That is not what happens in this play. This play is about two young lovers and their private lives—they are not highborn and neither has a "tragic flaw" or *hamartia*. *Romeo and Juliet* explores the problems faced by young people when they encounter rigidity from their parents and their society. One question this play raises is whether or not love can endure in an imperfect and tragic world. Romeo and Juliet do not bring the tragedy on themselves—it comes from the outside world and the rules and expectations of that outside world. Other important themes in this play include the relationship between parents and children, the honor code and revenge, the value of forgiveness, irrational violence and hatred, age versus youth, the self-knowledge that can evolve as one matures, and genuine love as opposed to infatuation or doting.

Until Act 3 and the death of Mercutio, this play teeters between tragedy and comedy and is filled with such comic elements as the absurdity of the servants, Romeo's affectations of being in love with Rosaline, Mercutio's mocking of serious things, the ridiculousness of the fathers' wanting to brawl, and the Nurse's unceasing flow of coarse, bawdy speech. Only after Mercutio's death does the play move toward tragic inevitability. Mercutio represents the imagination, the ability to see other ways of living, and, as "Mercury," the ancient messenger of the gods, the possibility of change and transformation. Once this power of possibility and imagination is removed from the play, authoritarianism, rigidity, and a failure of imagination on the part of the older generation doom both Romeo and Juliet.

One major theme in this play is the power of the past over the present. This theme fascinated Shakespeare and also figures prominently in later plays such as *Hamlet*. The past dominates the present here in the form of the feud between the Montagues and the Capulets. No one even knows why the families are feuding—the audience never finds out, and one is left with the sense that the feud is about the feud, the causes lost in the distant past. The feuding families of the play are unwilling to look at the feud critically, to question it in any way, or to try to resolve it, forgive, and move forward. The feud is simply the way things have always been and the way things are. This domination of the present by the past in Shakespeare almost always represents a failure of imagination, a failure of vision, as well as an inability to move forward into new ways of thinking and of being. This failure of vision is also seen in the language used in the play, and the way the language reinforces this theme. Often characters speak in clichéd, unthinking ways. Romeo's Petrarchanism at the beginning of the play illustrates this. Rather than experiencing love, he tries to force love into the popular clichés of the time.

The conflict between the generations, between youth and age, between children and their parents, is central to this play. Shakespeare uses this conflict to explore such issues as justice versus mercy and forgiveness, another favorite theme of Shakespeare's which he explored in other plays such as *The Merchant of Venice*. The theme of justice versus mercy is clearly seen in the Prince's decision to banish rather than execute Romeo after he has slain Tybalt.

Shakespeare uses the word "grace" to mean forgiveness as well as acceptance. "Grace" also refers to a world filled with God's forgiveness, love, and acceptance. The theme of grace and the importance of grace is presented in Act 2, scene 3 when Friar Lawrence gathers plants and says of these plants, in a speech that uses rhyme:

I must up-fill this osier cage of ours

With baleful weeds and precious-juiced flowers.

The earth that's nature's mother is her tomb;

What is her burying grave, that is her womb;

…

O, mickle is the powerful grace that lies

In plants, herbs, stones, and their true qualities;

For nought so vile that on the earth doth live

But to the earth some special good doth give;

Nor aught so good but, strain'd from that fair use,

Revolts from true birth, stumbling on abuse.

> Virtue itself turns vice, being misapplied,
>
> And vice sometime by action dignified.
>
> Within the infant rind of this weak flower
>
> Poison hath residence and medicine power;
>
> For this, being smelt, with that part cheers each part,
>
> Being tasted, stays all senses with the heart.
>
> Two such opposed kings encamp them still
>
> In man as well as herbs, grace and rude will;
>
> And where the worser is predominant,
>
> Full soon the canker death eats up that plant (2,3, 7-30).

This passage emphasizes that all things are given from God, but humans may use them in very different ways. The last four lines of this speech make an analogy, or comparison, between the world of plants and the world of humans. All humans, like all plants, have different sides to them—humans must face the conflict between grace (goodness, forgiveness, gentleness) and "rude will" (ego, self-interest, individual desire), and if the will is allowed to dominate, then a cancer will devour the individual just as it will the plant. This is the heart of *Romeo and Juliet*.

Even a love as perfect as theirs can be destroyed by the willful actions of parents and the older generation when they are eaten up by the cancer of hatred and can't forgive the past through an act of grace and move forward. Shakespeare's use of rhyme in the Friar's speech emphasizes the vision of God's world as harmonious and perfect. Both the poison used to feign Juliet's death and the poison Romeo used to kill himself were made from plants. Plants can purify and heal, or they can kill. All things are double in this world of contraries or opposites.

The honor code is another important theme in this play and another theme that Shakespeare would return to frequently in such plays as *Hamlet*. Shakespeare lived at the junction of two worlds—the medieval world and the modern world. The conflict between the honor code and a code of forgiveness is a central way Shakespeare explores these conflicts inherent in the old world view as it painfully gives birth to the new world of the Renaissance, and "renaissance" means "rebirth." All of us are familiar with the honor code since it still plays a part in the world we inhabit. One way of thinking about the difference between the honor code and a world based on forgiveness and grace is to imagine the honor code as something imposed from without—"this is what you should do and you aren't a man if you don't."

The world of forgiveness and grace is an interior world where the individual is motivated by conscience rather than the rules and expectations of others. An ethic of forgiveness builds a moral code that moves beyond the honor code and its emphasis on revenge. Acts of revenge create a cyclical world, a circular pattern in which an act demands revenge, which then demands revenge, which then demands revenge. This cycle of violence and retribution is one more example of a rigid and inflexible world.

This code of revenge, of honor, is a prison from which one cannot escape without imaginative acts of compassion, forgiveness, or transformation. This is the world that Tybalt and the other members of the Capulet and

Montague families inhabit. This is the world that Romeo and Juliet attempt to escape. They discover that they can only escape this world through death. One way of approaching their deaths is to view them as a sacrifice which eventually moves their families out of the cycle of revenge, out of the Old Testament morality of "an eye for an eye," and into the Christian world of forgiveness and grace. Shakespeare asks the audience to consider whether the dreadful sacrifice of these two young people is worth the end result. Have they redeemed this fallen world through their love and their deaths?

Shakespeare treats a wide variety of other themes in *Romeo and Juliet*. Love and the nature of love is central to this play. In *Romeo and Juliet*, Shakespeare seems to have written a play that emphasizes the possibility of "love at first sight" although in the companion play, *A Midsummer Night's Dream*, Shakespeare appears determined to tear that very theme apart and reveal how foolish a belief in love at first "sight" is.

Shakespeare explores the theme of "love" throughout this play and works to distinguish between a constructed vision of "romantic" love found in art and literature and the reality of love. He also contrasts mere infatuation with actual love throughout the play. One word that Shakespeare uses repeatedly in this play is "dote" or "doting," which is essentially what we think of today as infatuation. "Doting" is a superficial feeling and today contains the connotation of an indulgent parent or grandparent toward a child. Although Shakespeare presents the possibility of love at first sight in *Romeo and Juliet*, in *A Midsummer Night's Dream*, he questions whether or not "love at first sight" can lead to true love.

For Shakespeare, love is capable of working powerful transformations in those who truly love. In

Shakespeare's world, love is frequently associated with the imagination, and the ability to escape the prison of the self and to enter the mind and life of another through the act of deeply loving another. True, honest love is almost always an agent for change and growth in Shakespeare, while "romantic" love or infatuation actually prevents growth.

Romeo's development in the play illustrates this theme dramatically. When the play opens, he is a love-sick youth filled with fantasies of love. Romeo has a melancholic sensitivity, or humour, which he expresses in the clichéd and stilted language of Petrarchanism, but by the end of the play Romeo has stopped using elaborate, false, flowery language to describe his love and has moved toward straightforward, unadorned speech. After he learns of Juliet's "death" from Balthasar, he says,

Well, Juliet, I will lie with thee tonight.

Let's see for means. O mischief, thou art swift

To enter in the thoughts of despearate men! (5.1. 34-36).

Could Romeo make a more straightforward response than this? This is a plain way of speaking and, for Shakespeare, a more authentic way of speaking than the earlier high-blown and clichéd language Romeo used. Romeo, like Juliet, has been transformed and given courage by love.

Another theme in this play is gender and how our ideas of gender are constructed. Gender hasn't disappeared as an issue and is one that we continue to grapple with today; Shakespeare's exploration of this topic remains highly relevant to contemporary audiences. In *Romeo and Juliet*, Shakespeare is particularly concerned with the construction of maleness, although he also explores what it means to be a wife or a daughter. The focus, however, is on what it means to be a "man." Shakespeare uses the contrast between Tybalt and Romeo as his primary way of exploring this issue. Tybalt represents a more traditional construction of maleness. He is an old-fashioned hero who acts before thinking and is deeply concerned about such issues as reputation. Revenge is important to Tybalt as well. Characters such as Tybalt rarely come to good ends in Shakespeare. They represent the old, fading world of the classical past and the Middle Ages, a world that is, perhaps, heroic, but that doesn't fit the modern world and its changing times and ways of thinking.

Our first vision of Romeo is of a lovestruck, melancholy, and highly sensitive young man. This Romeo is not interested in such things as fighting or defending his honor or revenge. The Romeo we see at the beginning of the play can almost be visualized as a Renaissance "Emo" figure; he is soft, he is dreamy, and he hasn't yet had to confront the adult world with all of its demands, conflicts, responsibilities, and difficult choices.

After he kills Tybalt, Romeo falls apart, realizing the horror of his act and how he has succumbed to enacting a role expected of him, but one he did not value. In Act 3, Scene 3, both Friar Lawrence and the Nurse see him as womanly and "weak" and urge him to be a "man." The friar gives him such advice as to "arise," to "stand up" (3,3,71-75). This advice on what a man needs to be contains a bawdy dimension. When the Nurse enters, Friar Lawrence tells her that Romeo is "There on the ground, with his own tears made drunk" (3,3,83). The Nurse goes so far as to explicitly compare Romeo to Juliet:

> O, he is even in my mistress' case,
>
> Just in her case. O woeful sympathy!

> Piteous predicament! Even so lies she,
>
> Blubb'ring and weeping, weeping and blubb'ring.
>
> Stand up, stand up, stand, and you be a man.
>
> For Juliet's sake, for her sake, rise and stand;
>
> Why should you fall into so deep an O? (3, 3, 84-90).

Romeo immediately stands up after the Nurse addresses him. Several things are worth exploring in this short passage which demonstrate how Shakespeare can use language to present a layered and ambiguous scene. Romeo is being less than a man; he is, indeed, acting as Juliet is acting and is explicitly compared to a woman. The Nurse's use of the terms "stand up" and "rise and stand" call on Romeo to be virile and manly, and these words clearly contain sexual overtones of being upright and strong rather than impotent and unable to perform as a man "should." It's worth noting that "O" was also a slang term for a woman's sexual parts in the Renaissance. Clearly, a weeping, blubbering, impotent man is not a "man." Romeo threatens to end his life at this point, and Friar Lawrence says:

> Hold thy desperate hand!
>
> Art thou a man? Thy form cries out thou art;
>
> Thy tears are womanish, thy wild acts [denote]
>
> The unreasonable fury of a beast
>
> Unseemly woman in a seeming man,
>
> And ill-beseeming beast in seeming both,
>
> …

Thy noble shape is but a form of wax,

Digressing from the valor of a man; (3, 3, 108-127).

This scene ends with both the Friar and the Nurse making plans for Romeo to secretly meet Juliet in her room where the two lovers will consummate their marriage.

When he kills Tybalt, Romeo has just returned from his secret wedding to Juliet, and he tries very hard not to fight Tybalt. Mercutio steps in to duel Tybalt only because Mercutio is embarrassed for his friend, Romeo, and his apparent cowardice. When Mercutio steps forward to challenge Tybalt, he reinforces the power of traditional values such as the honor code. Throughout the play, Mercutio has been one of the most clear-sighted and cynical characters—a character who is able to see through the foolishness of social codes such as the formality and artificiality of Petrarchanism and the honor code. Under pressure, however, even Mercutio can succumb to his cultural programming.

Only after Mercutio's death does Romeo allow himself to be drawn into the honor code as well, and into the traditional vision of what it means to be a man. This code destroys Romeo, and the possibility of Romeo and Juliet being together, as well as taking Tybalt's life. Thus, Shakespeare leaves the audience with more questions than answers about what it means to be a man. One point Shakespeare seems to be making, though, is that such things as the self and gender are things that humans "perform" rather than actual real things. This idea still feels modern today. Our sense of ourselves as men or as women changes over the course of our lives and according to situation and context, so all of us find ourselves "performing" particular gender roles in different situations, roles such as "father," "cheerleader," "star athlete," "tough guy," "tomboy," "flirt," or even "dumb blond."

Shakespeare explores female roles primarily through Juliet, who challenges the roles offered to her by the other women in the play. The two mothers each assume a different traditional role, but both are subordinate to their husbands and in some sense represent weakness. Romeo's mother actually dies from grief when he is exiled, and Juliet's mother is unhappy in her marriage but still follows her husband's direction in all things. She even turns against Juliet to side with her husband when he arranges the marriage with Paris. The Nurse also betrays Juliet when she tells her to forget about Romeo and to marry Paris. In short, the women in the play are not consistently good to women, and their loyalty to fellow women falls away and is replaced by loyalty to the man in authority.

Juliet rejects all of these models for how women should behave, and the credit for this rejection of traditional roles has to go to the love she feels for Romeo—a love that takes her outside of herself and allows her to transcend traditional roles and beliefs. When we first meet Juliet, she is fulfilling a typical daughter's role. She is passive, submissive and willing to do whatever her parents tell her. She is not quite fourteen and appears willing to submit to parental authority. By the play's end, however, she has discovered herself and is no longer willing to be the submissive daughter. She takes action that subverts both her father and her mother. Juliet is clearly aware that gender roles are something humans perform; she compares herself explicitly to an actor playing a role in Act 4, Scene 3, when she states, "My dismal scene I needs must act alone" (4, 3, 19).

Time is another important theme in *Romeo and Juliet*—especially the theme of acting in haste. Everything in this play happens quickly and Friar Lawrence warns Romeo about the dangers of acting in haste. Everything that is done in haste, such as the marriage of Romeo and Juliet, the fight between Romeo and Tybalt, Juliet's father's attempts to push her into a marriage with Paris, and Romeo's response to the false report of Juliet's death, ends horribly. One could even argue that the imagery of poison which is so pervasive in this play is linked to the theme of hasty action. Friar Lawrence warns Romeo at the end of their first conversation not to act too hastily:

>   *Rom.* O, let us hence, I stand on sudden haste.

>   *Fri. L.* Wisely and slow, they stumble that run fast (2.3.93-94).

During the scene just before the marriage, this issue is again raised when Romeo urges Friar Lawrence to perform the marriage quickly, and Friar Lawrence responds:

>   These violent delights have violent ends,

>   And in their triumph die, like fire and powder,

>   Which as they kiss consume. The sweetest honey

>   Is loathsome in his own deliciousness,

>   And in the taste confounds the appetite.

>   Therefore love moderately: long love doth so;

>   Too swift arrives as tardy as too slow (2.5.9-15).

This theme of "violent delights have violent ends," was the theme or moral of the source Shakespeare used for *Romeo and Juliet*, but Shakespeare puts more focus on the joys of true love in this play, including physical love and physical pleasure.

Another theme in this play is the importance of coming to self-knowledge. One can only reach this self-knowledge alone and without the aid of others. Both Romeo and Juliet have to confront this failure of self-knowledge during the play. At the beginning of the play Romeo is in "love" with Rosaline, and Juliet's mother tells Juliet that she will soon be wed to Paris. Thus, each of our main characters finds him or herself in a false love relationship at the beginning of the play even though, in good Petrarchan fashion, neither has any real contact with the other "lover." Romeo and Juliet each have advisors in the play: Friar Lawrence for Romeo and the Nurse for Juliet. Each of these advisors fails to counsel them well when they are most in need of good advice. Shakespeare makes it clear that the path to self-knowledge is a journey that each of us must take on our own—alone and vulnerable.

The feud is central to this play, and the feud allows Shakespeare to focus on a number of themes that he also develops in other ways. A crucial point about this feud is that no one really remembers why the families are fighting. Shakespeare wrote repeatedly, especially in *Hamlet*, about the power of the past over the present, and about the necessity of leaving the past behind if one is going to move forward. The inability to move forward is present throughout this play. The only characters who demonstrate the ability to move beyond the past, Romeo and Juliet, are destroyed by the failure of their families to take that step as well.

The feud also represents the disastrous results of the honor code with its emphasis on reciprocal action—kind of like the "he hit me first" we used to whine about when we were small children. No one is going to stop hitting the other until one person decides to stop or until an authority figure steps in.

Unfortunately, in this play the authority figure turns out to be powerless to stop the constant brawling. This honor code puts a great emphasis on revenge. Revenge can be visualized as a rigid code, a code that feeds on itself, a code that will continue infinitely into the future until people like Romeo and Juliet are willing to push aside old grievances and transform the evils of the past into the blessings of the future. The world of *Romeo and Juliet* has no room for this transformation. The death of Mercutio in Act 3, the one character other than the two central figures of Romeo and Juliet, who has flexibility and imagination, makes anything other than the tragic ending impossible.

Romeo and Juliet, contains many other themes such as the role of fate or fortune in human destiny. Explore these ideas more deeply as a way of extending your understanding and appreciation of this play. Some themes you might also want to spend time with include parents, children and their relationships with each other, and whether children have something to teach the parents as well as the other way around; the nature of hatred, especially irrational hatred, and the effects of hatred on the one who hates as well as the one who is hated; contrasts between age and youth; the benefits and drawbacks of a flexible approach to life as opposed to a rigid one; and the differences between a life lived according to the code of honor and revenge as opposed to a life lived according to the principles of charity and forgiveness.

Language and Poetic Conventions

Petrarch (Francisco Petrarcho, 1304-1374) was one of the creators of Italian Humanism, which helped lay the groundwork for the Renaissance. Today, as well as during Shakespeare's time, he is most remembered as the creator of a lyric poetry tradition that has come to be called Petrarchanism.

At the age of 23 Petrarch saw a woman with whom he supposedly fell deeply in love, even though this was the only time he saw her and he never had any actual contact with her. Petrarch celebrated this woman, whom he named "Laura," in a series of poems that were later collected in a collection of 366 poems called *Il Canzoniere* (*The Song Book*). In these poems Petrarch helped create the sonnet form as a poem devoted to love, and the theme of the ideal, but unattainable, love. Petrarch did not invent the sonnet, nor did he invent the conventions of courtly love. He did make both wildly popular. The sonnet pattern that Petrarch developed follows the usual fourteen lines of rhymed iambic pentameter that characterizes all sonnets. The Petrarchan, or Italian, sonnet has two divisions, the octet or octave, the first eight lines, and the sestet, the last six lines. Typically the poet will develop a problem in the octet and resolve that problem in the sestet. The usual rhyme scheme is *abbaabba* for the octet and *cdecde* or *cdcdcd* for the sestet.

The English poets Sir Thomas Wyatt and Henry Howard introduced the sonnet to England in the mid 16th century, although they modified the Italian sonnet in ways that created what is known as the English or Shakespearean sonnet, even though Shakespeare did not create this form. The English sonnet typically has three quatrains (four-line stanzas) and a concluding rhymed couplet (two lines). Often the first twelve lines of the English sonnet will be devoted to elaborating a problem and the concluding couplet will resolve that problem. Don't get too bound up with these definitions. The seventeenth century English poet John Milton wrote one of the best examples of the Italian sonnet in his sonnet, "When I Consider How My Light Is Spent." Shakespeare himself used the Italian form at times, so the English versus Petrarchan sonnet distinction is largely academic.

Sonnets are traditionally written as a sequence, or series of poems, celebrating the beauty or desirability of a particular woman. The sonnet became highly fashionable during the sixteenth century in England, and many poets wrote sonnet sequences celebrating the beauty of their love, or the desirability of their love, or the religion of love, which meant they treated love as though it were a kind of religion. In one sonnet the poet might celebrate his love's eyes, and in another he might describe the pleasures he would like to share with his love.

This Petrarchan approach to love became a powerful fad in late sixteenth century England and eventually gave rise to an anti-Petrarchan counter movement which might talk about a loved one's unattractiveness or unworthiness. Many of Shakespeare's sonnets are in this anti-Petrarchan mode, and the play *Romeo and Juliet* is, in many ways, an anti-Petrarchan play. As the audience watches Romeo change from the affected and melancholic Petrarchan lover to a man who experiences the depth of true love in his relationship with Juliet, the silliness of these conventions becomes clear.

These Petrarchan sonnets were highly rhetorical and made use of complex linguistic strategies such as antithesis, paradox, oxymoron, and puns.

Some Typical Tropes or Figures of Speech in *Romeo and Juliet*

Antithesis is a figure of speech which uses an opposition or contrast of ideas; usually this juxtaposition of opposites is expressed through the parallelism of words that mean different things such as "the beloved enemy" of this play. Antithesis and **oxymoron** are closely related figures of speech. Act 3, Scene 2 offers some brilliant examples of antithesis in the following speech from Juliet after she learns that Romeo has killed Tybalt:

O serpent heart, hid with a flowering face!

Did ever dragon keep so fair a cave?

Beautiful tyrant! fiend angelical!

Dove-feather'd raven! wolvish-ravening lamb!

Despised substance of divinest show!

Just opposite to what thou justly seem'st,

A damned saint, an honourable villain!

> O nature, what hadst thou to do in hell,
>
> When thou didst bower the spirit of a fiend
>
> In mortal paradise of such sweet flesh?
>
> Was ever book containing such vile matter
>
> So fairly bound? O that deceit should dwell
>
> In such a gorgeous palace! (3.2.73-84).

This entire speech is filled with antitheses. The opening image of the "serpent heart hid with a flowering face," for example, sets up an opposition between interior and exterior in which a beautiful and innocent appearance hides a deceptive and evil interior. Other examples of this figure of speech from the first lines include the dragon in a beautiful cave, the appealing tyrant, and the fiend who appears to be an angel. Shakespeare continues this use of antithesis throughout the speech.

An **oxymoron** is a figure of speech which combines contradictory terms to create an effect such as ambiguity. *Romeo and Juliet* is filled with examples of oxymoron such as "the beloved enemy," but an even better example occurs in Act 1, Scene 1, in Romeo's speech:

> Here's much to do with hate, but more with love.
>
> Why then, O brawling love! O loving hate!
>
> O anything! Of nothing first create!
>
> O heavy lightness! Serious vanity!
>
> Mis-shapen chaos of well [-seeming] forms! (1.1.175-79).

When Romeo refers to "brawling love," and "loving hate," he is making use of oxymora (the plural form of oxymoron). Not only does this create a sense of ambiguity, but it points to the paradoxes hidden in both love and hate. If one feels an intense hatred for someone, for example, does that hatred demand the same sort of focus on the enemy that intense love demands for the beloved?

Paradox is usually thought of as a contradictory statement which seems meaningless at first but on further examination turns out to contain a deep truth which sometimes brings the oppositions into balance. In the New Testament Jesus says to his followers that in order to save their lives, they must lose their lives. He is telling his followers that in order to attain salvation and eternal life after death, they must leave their old life with its worldly concerns behind. Perhaps the most famous paradox in *Romeo and Juliet* occurs in Act 2, Scene 3, lines 183-5:

Yet I shall kill thee with much cherishing.

Goodnight, goodnight! Parting is such sweet sorrow

That I shall say goodnight till it be morrow.

Why would parting be sweet? Is it because of the anticipation that the speaker will feel for the next meeting? How can sorrow be sweet?

Puns are a figure of speech involving a play on words; typically a word will be used in a way that calls up more than one meaning of the word at the same time or recalls a word that sounds similar but means something entirely different. Puns are also called "quibbles," and these were among Shakespeare's favorite figures of speech. Many readers find these puns to be among Shakespeare's most endearing qualities. A famous example from *Romeo and*

Juliet occurs when Mercutio makes the following comment as he is dying:

> Ask for me tomorrow and you shall find me a **grave** man (3.1.98).

He will be "grave" not only because he will no longer be making jokes, but also because he will be dead and buried in a grave—obviously a serious matter. Another example occurs in the first scene of the play:

> Sampson: Gregory, o' my word, we'll not carry **coals**
>
> Gregory: No, for then we should be **colliers**
>
> Sampson: I mean, an [if] we be in **choler**, we'll draw
>
> Gregory: Ay, while you live, draw your neck out o' the **collar**

The puns here emphasize coals (which burn), colliers (who deliver coal), and choler, which means anger. Shakespeare has great fun with these puns that emphasize heat, fire, and anger, but then brings the fun to an incongruous close with a pun on "collar" or a noose that would be used to hang a person.

Petrarchanism and the Petrarchan Tradition

Shakespeare uses the Petrarchan tradition as a source of comedy in the first acts of *Romeo and Juliet*. Romeo is the traditional Petrarchan lover, and Leonard Foster has argued that the entire play is designed to bring the

Petrarchan cliché of the "dear enemy" to life. This cliché is also an example of an oxymoron, as is the later combination, "cold fire." The Petrarchan tradition made frequent use of oxymoron to emphasize the contradictory nature of love. Another aspect of the Petrarchan tradition that Shakespeare is satirizing in the character of Romeo is the symbolic representation of love as a religion. This play is drenched in religious imagery. When Romeo meets Juliet at the masquerade, for instance, he is dressed as a "palmer" or pilgrim, and the first conversation between the two lovers uses religious imagery throughout. Romeo refers to Juliet's hand as a "shrine" and her lips as "pilgrims." Juliet calls Romeo a "pilgrim." Their first kiss is referred to as a prayer.

A further example of Shakespeare playing with Petrarchan tradition is how he makes lavish use of the sonnet form in *Romeo and Juliet*. The play itself begins with a sonnet as the prologue, a sonnet that includes many of the image patterns and themes that will later unfold in the play. Our introduction to Romeo includes a sonnet that he speaks in the Petrarchan style (1.1.168-74).

This sonnet is filled with the empty language of Petrarchanism and images such as "sick health and the previously mentioned "cold fire." In the opening of the play, Romeo is "in love" with Rosaline, but this love reveals itself as nothing more than a cliché from Petrarchanism. Romeo is an infatuated weakling at the beginning of the play, and, as we have established, one of the things he has to do during the course of the play is discover the true meaning of love, which leads him toward self-knowledge. When we first see him, he is lovesick, a lover who has placed his love, Rosaline, on a pedestal, a lover who is really in love with the idea of himself being in love. By the end of the play he has matured and come to understand what love really is. In fact, one could argue that the rapid maturing that occurs in the space of just a few days is due to Romeo coming to understand love. That is the power of seeing someone else as equal to and connected to one's deepest self, purpose, and value—learning to love deeply helps us to access our emotional depths. Romeo now knows what love truly is and cannot find a way to survive in a world without this love.

The audience can still see Romeo's immaturity in what he does next. Yes, he is now a more mature and thoughtful young man. His love for Juliet has shown him that many of the beliefs and traditions with which he was raised and to which he was once loyal—the "us" versus "them" mentality that pits members of one family against another across generations—are false. These false ideals of family and honor promote the false values of suspicion, hatred, and discrimination based on family. They are antithetical to love, and the lead to a range of emotions and behaviors that are an opposition to love: fear, dueling, treachery, and death.

If Romeo had been more mature and wiser, he, as well as Juliet, would not have acted so rashly, so suddenly, or in such extreme ways. Real love goes beyond learning to love a single person, that obsessive focus on a special one who in turn makes us special, cocoons us from life's hardships, and can even lead to its own smaller version of "us vs. them." Even with Juliet's dramatic act of taking a draught to feign death, if Romeo had allowed himself to grieve, to sit with his pain and loss and even to feel that side of love, rather than rushing to escape from intense pain into death, he would have known, and earned, a deeper understanding of what it means to love someone, and he would have been able to build a life with Juliet after she had awakened. But that would have been a different play entirely, and *Romeo and Juliet* is a tragedy and so demands the death of the hero and heroine.

In *Romeo and Juliet* Shakespeare establishes himself as an anti-Petrarchan, and one of the sources of enjoyment in this play is to watch Romeo as the heart-sick, love-sick Petrarchan lover—drowning in melancholy and in love with an idealized vision of woman rather than a real woman, with a fantasy rather than the complicated truth.

Imagery

One of the most important elements in all of Shakespeare's plays is his use of **imagery**. The images that recur in a particular play can provide great insight into the play and its themes. Imagery refers to the use of language to represent such things as emotions, thoughts, objects, or any sort of physical, emotional, or mental state or experience. Most imagery is found in figurative language such as **metaphor** or **simile**. These figures of speech are frequently referred to as "tropes." This word is a sort of umbrella term used for any kind of figurative or non-literal use of language. The word "trope" comes from the Greek word "tropos" and means "to turn." Figurative language often "turns" language or imagery in ways that give the audience new insights or new ways of thinking about a word or image. In literary studies, a trope can refer to any kind of figurative language such as metaphor or simile.

Metaphor is perhaps the most common form of trope, and, like any writer or speaker of English, Shakespeare uses metaphor constantly. Metaphor has fascinated students of language and linguistics and during the last few decades has been the focus of intense study and research—especially from scholars such as cognitive linguists, who study connections between human language and human thought and relationships between language and the brain. The word "metaphor" derives from the Greek word "*metaphoros*," which means "to transfer," and that's what metaphor does—it transfers the meaning of one word or concept to another. Metaphor is traditionally defined as an unstated comparison of two things as in "She lights up the room with her smile" or "that baby's a doll." Students of language point out that metaphor is more than just a figure of speech. One of the reasons metaphor has received so much attention during the last forty years is that scholars have realized that metaphor is one of the basic ways that language itself works. Many of our most common statements in English are based on metaphor. If someone is told to keep her "eye on the prize" or that his "pen is on fire," he or she is dealing with metaphors. A typical example of metaphor in *Romeo and Juliet* occurs when Juliet's mother is describing Paris and says:

> Read o'er the volume of young Paris' face,
>
> And find delight writ there with beauty's pen;
>
> Examine every married lineament,
>
> And see how one another lends content;
>
> And what obscur'd in this fair volume lies
>
> Find written in the margent of his eyes.
>
> This precious book of love, this unbound lover,
>
> To beautify him, only lacks a cover (1.3.81-88).

Here again, Shakespeare is undercutting the literary tradition of Petrarchanism. The metaphor here is of Paris as a book, written by beauty's pen, filled with content (with a pun on contentment), provided with margins for someone to write notes upon, but still not bound together as a whole. All

The Make It Fun Guide to Romeo and Juliet

Paris needs is the cover, the binding, and Juliet will provide that. The word "married" in this passage is also a metaphor, and refers to how the features of his face (lineament) are joined together (married) in a pleasing fashion.

A **Simile** is an explicit comparison which typically uses the words "like" or "as" to announce the comparison. Such common expressions as, "That baby's as cute as a button," or "he's crazy as a look," or "sly like a fox" are similes. Similes express "similarities" and are essentially a logical form of expression. The speaker or writer announces the comparison. This announcement of the comparison is the main way that simile differs from metaphor.

This is quite different from metaphor where the comparison is simply made but not announced—where meaning is transferred from one idea or concept or image to another. Metaphor taps into our deeper ways of thinking and imagining while simile works with our more rational mind. Similes, like metaphors, are everywhere in *Romeo and Juliet*. In Act 4, Scene 1, Shakespeare uses both metaphor and simile when Friar Lawrence describes to Juliet what the effects of his potion will be:

> No warmth, no [breath] shall testify thou livest;
>
> The roses in thy lips and cheeks shall fade
>
> To [wanny] ashes, thy eyes' windows fall,
>
> Like death when he shuts up the day of life;
>
> Each part, depriv'd of supple government,
>
> Shall, stiff and stark and cold, appear like death (4.2.98-103).

The similes here are those comparisons that begin with "like."

The metaphors in this passage include comparing Juliet's lips and cheeks to roses and her eyes to windows that have been closed. The similes include the falling of the windows of her eyes "like death when he shuts up the day of life, her limbs being stiff and cold "like death."

Shakespeare is a master at using repeated images drawn from a particular field of meaning such as "night" or "fire" or "birds" to create patterns of images that reinforce the characters, plot, and meaning of his plays. Some of the important image patterns in *Romeo and Juliet* include eyes (often with an accompanying pun on "I"), hands, darkness and light, flowers and buds, canker (cancer), poison, plants, death, plague, infection, pestilence, pilgrims, falcons and birds, time (especially images of haste), books, "wax," and a variety of bawdy imagery. Bawdy imagery is imagery that has a sexual dimension to it. Earlier we explored some of the ways that Shakespeare makes use of "hand" imagery, and how this hand imagery accentuates the various ways hands can be used such as for brawling, for loving, for caressing, or for joining in marriage. This use of the image of hands in a variety of ways emphasizes the complexity of our connections to ideas, to the world around us, and to our relationships with each other.

The images of light are often fiery, even violent, such as those involving lightning and gunpowder, but light imagery in *Romeo and Juliet* also include references to radiant light, sunshine, starlight, moonbeams, sunrise and sunset, the sparkle of fire, a meteor, candles, torches, quick-coming darkness, clouds, mist, rain, and night. Astronomical imagery of the sun, moon, and stars also link to light, as does some of the elemental imagery using images of earth, air, fire, and water.

This light imagery serves a variety of purposes. For instance images of brief, explosive light in a dark landscape are used with such images as lightning or explosions of gunpowder. This brief light illuminates for an instant a landscape that is otherwise dark and forbidding. This brief illumination is precisely what the love of Romeo and Juliet provides their families—a brief glimpse of a world that exists in the darkness of hatred and feuds. This imagery also illuminates the nature of young love with its intensity and often brevity. The violent images of light such as gunpowder and lightning are frequently associated with the intensity of the love shared by Romeo and Juliet. These images of explosive light in the darkness emphasize the brilliant, yet brief, nature of the love shared by Romeo and Juliet.

Light imagery also connects the audience to the natural world and reminds the audience that its members are part of a natural order of things, not separate from the rising and setting of the sun and the moon, the seasons, or cycles of life and death. Remember that early and sudden death was commonplace in Shakespeare's time. The Bubonic Plague, known as the Black Death, struck England once again in 1592-1593, killing over 10,000 people in London alone and closing the theaters for a year. Shakespeare lost family members and other people he knew from the plague and other illnesses.

The lives of people of Shakespeare's era could be extinguished at any time. Therefore, Shakespeare seems to suggest that it is best to burn brightly, to live fully, during the flash of light in which we live our lives. We cannot fully overcome the difficulty and darkness of the world around us, but we can choose to shine, to shed a bit of light, over the course of our brief stay in this world.

Almost all of the important scenes in *Romeo and Juliet* take place at night or in darkness, a setting that is at once romantic, yet obscure, emphasizing the themes of the play and its tragic conclusion. The two lovers provide a possibility of light in this darkness, and often these images of light are associated with the two lovers, as in the balcony scene (2.2) where images of the moon and the sun are developed in great detail.

Shakespeare reverses the way that images of the sun and the moon have traditionally been used in art. During Shakespeare's time the sun was usually associated with men, and the moon with women. This association illustrated traditional ideas about gender roles since the sun was associated with constancy or loyalty in love, and the moon was associated with inconstancy or lack of loyalty in love. The moon changed every night, and this was associated with the Renaissance view that women were not as "constant" as men. Other reasons for the association of the moon with women were that it "shone" because of the reflected light of the sun, it had a twenty-eight day cycle, as does a woman, and it was supposed to be the home of the muse, of inspiration. In Act 2, Scene 2, Romeo says

> Lady, by yonder blessed moon I vow,
>
> That tips with silver all these fruit-tree tops—

And Juliet interrupts him to say,

> O, swear not by the moon, th' inconstant moon,
>
> That monthly changes in her [circled] orb,
>
> Lest that thy love prove likewise variable (107-111).

Since men are associated with the sun and constancy, his desire to swear by the moon reflects this reversal that Shakespeare is developing. Juliet does not want him to swear by the moon since it is inconstant and always changing. She wants him to be true to her and not to vary in his love.

The images of plants are developed overtly in Friar Lawrence's speech on the properties of plants (2.3.1-30). This speech also emphasizes the elemental imagery of earth, air, fire, and water. In this speech the audience learns that, thanks to the nature of the universe and its regular cycles of day and night, of birth, death, and decay, one is able to see the grace of God as it works in the world, even though it is a world of mutability, decay, and death. The earth gives both poisonous plants and medicinal flowers, and the same plant may contain both poison and medicine. These fundamental laws also apply to humans who can use their lives to try to do the right thing or to be harmful.

Flower imagery is also applied to Juliet. Shakespeare gives the plant imagery associated with Juliet mythic resonance by using this imagery to link her with the mythic story of Prosperina, Persephone in Greek, the daughter of Ceres who was kidnapped by Pluto and taken to the underworld. Ceres, from whose name we get the word "cereal," introduced plowing and farming to humankind and gave humans the gift of grain as well as the gift of law. Ceres searched desperately for her daughter after she disappeared. Eventually Ceres learned the truth about Prosperina, that she had become Queen of the Underworld. Ceres went to Jupiter and demanded the return of her daughter. Jupiter agreed on one condition: no morsel of food could have passed her lips while in Hades. Unfortunately, Prosperina had eaten seven pomegranate seeds while in Hades. Jupiter resolved the conflict between Pluto and Ceres by dividing the year into equal parts and Prosperina, the only divinity common to both the world above ground and the world below, would spend six months on earth, spring and summer, when plants would grow, and six months in

Hades, autumn and winter when the world would be cold, dark, and not bear fruit.

Like Prosperina, Juliet is associated with flowers, and spends time in the underworld while still alive, just as Juliet does after she drinks the potion Friar Lawrence gave her. Prosperina was kidnapped because Cupid had pierced Pluto with one of his arrows of love, and Jupiter told Ceres at one point that Pluto had committed no crime, but only an act of love, and so should not be punished. This ancient myth parallels the story of Romeo and Juliet, who are also motivated by love. While Juliet also spends time in the underworld, in this tragedy there is no rebirth or emergence from the darkness of the tomb. Both Romeo and Juliet become citizens of the underworld for all time.

Yet, in a way, their love does transform the world they left behind, does bring a kind of springtime and harvest for those who follow. Only by being forced to confront their rigidity, hatred, and folly when confronted by the greatest loss possible are the families driven to stop feuding. Each family has lost its only children, and so their future is lost as well. They have no legacy.

Still, hatred is replaced by the possibility of love, of compassion, of healing from past wrongs, from the sins committed in the past. The families do come together after the deaths of Romeo and Juliet as the two families swear to forget their feud and raise golden statues to remember their children and their love.

Activities

One of the most fascinating aspects of Shakespeare is that he is constantly fresh, becoming new and different for each generation. The plays remain the same, but each generation recreates Shakespeare and finds elements in Shakespeare that speak to that generation and that time. This constant newness is part of Shakespeare's magic. Each generation finds a perspective on his plays that speak to them and for them. The activities that follow try to bring Shakespeare alive for twenty-first century readers. These activities should also help you reach a greater understanding of the play and its characters.

Make It Fun guides are different from most study guides for topics such as *Romeo and Juliet*. Instead of offering things like questions to write essays about or discussion questions for a class period, book club, or study group, we have tried to develop a variety of activities that will make the reading of the play more enjoyable. Some of the following activities are for individuals, some are for groups, and all will be helpful to readers of Shakespeare, including teachers or students, in developing a deeper understanding of the play.

Explore these activities and bring different approaches to them as you think about *Romeo and Juliet*.

1. One of the most interesting ways to approach this highly "musical" play is to try different musical approaches to it. You might try delivering the verse as "rap" songs or with a hip hop rhythm. You might want to try reading some of the sonnets from the play as if you were giving a slam poetry reading.

Watching the musical *West Side Story* is a good way to start thinking about this play from a musical point-of-view. Baz Luhrman's movie, *Romeo + Juliet*, presents the party at the Capulet house as though it were a contemporary rave. Can you visualize or create doo-wop or psychedelic or punk or reggae versions of segments of the play? Parts of *Romeo and Juliet* could be lifted straight from country and western music. How might you create a "twang" version of a scene? An Emo version? A Rockabilly version?

Create a short version of the play that keeps all the essential elements of the plot, but recasts the plot using contemporary characters and character types and is rewritten to the rhythm of rap or hip-hop. In other words, who would Tybalt be today? A colleague at a law firm? A check out clerk at a grocery store? Recast the characters into modern roles and attitudes. What about the Nurse? Is she an aunt, a neighbor, a teacher, a talk show host? Try this same process with other characters such as Romeo, Juliet, or Mercutio.

2. Imagine the imagery: One of the best ways to exercise your imagination with these plays is to spend some time thinking about the imagery. For instance, Shakespeare often uses imagery of bright and brief light illuminating darkness. In *Romeo and Juliet* these include images of lightning and the explosion of gunpowder. Why does he use this kind of imagery in this play about teenagers in love facing enormous obstacles from the outside world? Try doing a five-minute free write exploring this image. Why do

The Make It Fun Guide to Romeo and Juliet

so many of the scenes in *Romeo and Juliet* take place at night?

Choose another image pattern to explore. Important image patterns in this play are built around plants, disease, poison, astrology, the humours, religion, falconry, birds, music, and books. Try to think about why Shakespeare chose these particular images and what these image patterns add to the play.

3. Youtube has an enormous variety of "versions" of *Romeo and Juliet*. Watch a few of these and then create your own version of the play or a scene in the play to act out or to post on Youtube. Maybe the Nurse loves clips of "cute" kittens. Mercutio might like the parody versions of such things as Gangnam style on Youtube. What if Romeo and Tybalt fought with light sabers? What if *Romeo and Juliet* attended a particular high school or college?

4. Write an obituary for Romeo, Juliet, Mercutio or Tybalt. What important elements of each character would you stress if you were trying to sum up Romeo or Juliet's life in fewer than 250 words?

5. Create a storyboard for a scene: storyboards are the visualizations that film and television producers use to help them "see" a scene before it is filmed. Choose a scene from the play and turn that scene into a storyboard that illustrates where characters would be positioned while speaking, what the setting would be like, what the costumes would be like, and how the characters would move during the scene. You might want to use a posterboard and create a series of drawings that illustrate the parts of the scene and how you envision it being performed.

6. Create a poster for the play, a scene or a character that captures the essence of the scene or the character. Is the

poster flat, a typical two-dimensional design? What if your "poster" for the play were a stature, a diorama, a small sculpture or a multi-media piece?

7. Create a billboard advertising a modern version of *Romeo and Juliet*. What would be the most important thing to emphasize in this billboard? What aspect of the play would this modern production stress? Would it be the gang-like quality of the violence? The conflict between parents and children? Revenge?

8. Develop a computer presentation using Prezi or Microsoft PowerPoint or Apple Keynote or any other kind of presentation software. Choose one scene for the play and develop a series of eight to ten slides that develop the most important elements of the scene. Be sure to include brief text for each slide that explains what is happening in your slide.

9. A vision board is an interesting exercise. In vision boards, people clip photos from magazines, the Internet, or other sources and create a poster that represents all the things they hope for in life. What would a poster creating the dreams and goals of any of the major (or minor) characters include? Apps that help you create a vision board that combines images found online with text that you write yourself. Create a vision board on a poster or as an electronic photo gallery for one of the characters in the play.

10. Translate characters or scenes or the entire play into contemporary situations that involve love, melancholy, parent/child conflict. How many of you know someone whose parents have forbidden them to go out with a specific person? How many of you have ever crashed a party in the way that Mercutio, Romeo, and Benvolio do? Have any of your friends ever moaned and groaned about an individual they were "in love" with, creating an imaginary relationship

The Make It Fun Guide to Romeo and Juliet

that lived only in fantasy and the mind? Do you know any Rosalines or young Romeos?

11. What kind of music would one of the major characters in the play listen to? Does Romeo like independent rock? What about Juliet? Is she a fan of music aimed at thirteen-year-olds today? Would Mercutio prefer reggae or grunge? Does Tybalt like death metal or rap? How about the Nurse? Does she like country and western songs. Try to create a music mix of seven to ten songs that captures the personality of one of the major characters.

If you were to classify other types of music, such as hiphop, country, opera, and pop, which humour would you associate with each one? How would you justify your choice?

12. Use either online images and photos or your own photos to create a visual slide show for one of the characters. Can you capture the essence of Romeo, Juliet, Mercutio, Tybalt, Friar Lawrence, or the Nurse in a set of images that use no words at all? What kinds of images would you choose for a character? Why would you choose these? Would someone viewing your slideshow know which character the slide show depicts? What images would give the character away? What kinds of visual symbols would you select to represent this character?

13. Select a current or recent popular television series such as *Glee*, *Friends*, *Mad Men*, *True Blood*, or *Breaking Bad*, and assign characters from the series you choose as parallels to key characters from *Romeo and Juliet*. Who will be Romeo? How would Romeo's character be like the one you've chosen and how would Romeo change? What would this new Romeo be like? Would he act differently than he does in the play? Would he think differently? Would he have new or different insights and

133

wisdom? Would he have new character flaws and obstacles to overcome?

14. Be a mime. Mimes have to convey the meaning of a situation without words and only through movement and facial expression. Choose one scene or situation in *Romeo and Juliet* and perform it as a mime. Acting as a mime involves a purely physical repertoire or set of actions and facial expressions. How does stripping a scene of its words change how the audience interprets it? Is the comedy and humor in a scene more apparent? Does the tragedy loom larger in the audience's mind?

15. Charades for various scenes work very well. Write up note cards that specify a scene or a key piece of dialogue in the play and work in groups to develop and perform charades for others to try to figure out.

16. Do you know anyone who has a clichéd vision of love today—anyone who is love with love? Create a scene between two friends using this theme in a contemporary way. Do we have clichéd approaches to love such as the Petrarchanism of the Renaissance? Try to list some of the clichés about love people use today.

17. Examine some recent films aimed at a female audience. Sometimes these films are referred to in a slightly derogatory way as "chick flicks" or as "RomComs." What sorts of parallels between these movies can you find in terms of plot (story line), character, or theme? Do these movies always have a happy ending? What about romantic movies that end in tragedy?

18. Try to uncover the formula for thee kinds of movies. Is there just one pattern, or are there two or three? How are they the same? How do they differ? Shakespeare also followed a sequence in the development of his play,

beginning with the set up of the characters, themes, and plot in a largely comedic vein, then providing a turning point, or pivot, and the resulting tragedy that unfolds. Choose a "chick flick" movie and divide it into scenes. Name each scene and list the story elements that are present. For example, Scene 1 could be "boy meets girl," and Scene 2 could demonstrate the character flaws of the major characters. These flaws might be things such as arrogance, narcissism, pride, or fear of intimacy. In Scene 3, the main characters might confront an obstacle to their being together such as friends or family who oppose the relationship for reason such as distrust or class. Another scene might focus on the character of a friend of one of the lead characters.

Go back to *Romeo and Juliet* and try using the same approach. Give a title to each scene. List at least four essential aspects of the story such as character, them, plot, setting, or imagery, and explore how these are introduced or explored in this scene. How is each element essential to the play as a whole? What does each element contribute? How does each element move the story forward in some way?

19. Could you explore the plot, themes, and character from recent books such as *The Hunger Games* or *The Fault in Our Stars*? Try to find the literary conventions in contemporary romantic comedies and tragicomedies. Can you find parallels with *Romeo and Juliet*? What are some of the differences that you notice in contemporary treatments of these characters, plots, or storylines? Literary genres follow the conventions or expectations for that particular literary style, letting audiences know what to expect from a particular type of story. Are these expectations comforting to the reader or viewer? What happens when these conventions are broken in a movie such as *Bridesmaids*?

20. Look for examples of foreshadowing in *Romeo and Juliet*. Foreshadowing in a work of literature is when a

writer hints at things that will occur later in a work of art such as a play. When Romeo expresses concerns about crashing the party at the Capulet house in Act 1, Scene 4 of the play, his fears foreshadow future events in the play. He worries that if they enter the house, some preordained fate determined by the stars will start to play out which will end in his death. Can you find other examples of foreshadowing in *Romeo and Juliet*? Why does think Shakespeare use this literary technique? Does foreshadowing help the play hold together? Does it help prepare the audience for what is coming?

How you ever experienced "foreshadowing" in your own life? Do you ever get a sense of inevitability about things that are going to occur in your life? Do you ever have a sense of an action that you've taken leading inevitability to a specific result or conclusion? Think back on your life to find an event that was foreshadowed in some way before it occurred.

21. *Romeo and Juliet* Jeopardy is a fun way to get to know the details of this play. What about other game shows? How might they work with *Romeo and Juliet*? Try creating a *Romeo and Juliet Wheel of Fortune* or *Newlywed Game* or *Family Feud*.

22. Stereotyping: Try to develop one-word descriptions of each of the major characters. We all know that stereotyping is bad, but we all also know that stereotyping is a fact of life. What one-word stereotype could be used for either set of parents? For Romeo? For Juliet? For Mercutio? For Tybalt? For the Nurse? What do these stereotypical labels reveal about the characters in *Romeo and Juliet*? Since stereotypes can both conceal and reveal, what aspects of a character's personality do these labels conceal or make difficult for an audience to see?

23. Almost all of us have to deal with the dreams our parents have for us as opposed to what we ourselves want out of life. Write a diary entry for Juliet (or any other character) expressing that character's feelings about this conflict.

24. Try acting out a particular scene from the play. This activity demands that you think deeply about the characters each actor will represent, and bringing the play to life through speech, gesture, and actions. Try acting out a scene such as Romeo and Juliet meeting or the balcony. The duels between Tybalt and Mercutio and later between Romeo and Tybalt also work well. Try one of the scenes that features the nurse. The death scene of Romeo and Juliet is fascinating, and if you want to have some fun, explore the scenes where either Romeo or Juliet are responding to the death of Tybalt. Trying to portray the early Romeo and his infatuation with Rosaline is an interesting exploration of "love" and character. The conflict between Juliet and her parents over her initial refusal to marry the County Paris could have been lifted from many contemporary households with parents trying to guide and mold their children's choices along expected or acceptable lines.

25. A *tableau vivant* (living picture) is the attempt to use living people to recreate a famous painting or work of art. "Actors" are posed with one another, sometimes in costume, sometimes holding props, to create a "snapshot" that evokes a painting or an entire scene of a play. Try creating a *tableau vivant* for a scene or situation in *Romeo and Juliet*.

26. As you were reading about the Renaissance theory of the humours, did you think about how this could be applied today? Do you know anyone who seems to a victim of melancholy or whose primary characteristic is anger (choler) or optimism (sanguine) or even lethargy and

the difficulty of getting things done (phlegm). Try using the humours to create psychological profiles of people you know—friends, teachers, parents, siblings. Shakespeare uses the humour of melancholy as a way of satirizing Romeo's being in love with love.

27. Invent a "humour" of your own to describe a characteristic mood, attitude, and outlook you've observed in people. What is the name of this new "humour"? Which "element" or bodily fluid is this humour associated with? Don't confine yourself to the four elements of earth, water, air, and fire, or even to the scientific elements such as hydrogen and carbon that we have today, but think about other aspects of our world and how these might be elements. What would a person whose primary "humour" was linked to an "element" such as wood be like? What if a person's primary "humour" was linked to lead, gold, mercury, plastic, or stainless steel? Could you apply this new "humour" to one of the characters in *Romeo and Juliet*?

28. One of the interesting things about the humours is that at different times various humours became fashionable. Melancholy was a "fashionable" humour when Shakespeare was writing *Romeo and Juliet*, and it was also fashionable two hundred years later at the end of the eighteenth century. This latter time period is sometimes referred to as the "Age of Sensibility" since so many people were using the melancholy stance to show how they were more sensitive than anyone else. The German writer Johann Goethe's popular book, *The Sorrows of Young Werther*, comes from this time period. The Brontë sisters' novels, *Wuthering Heights* and *Jane Eyre* are filled with melancholic characters such as Heathcliff. What about today? Which of the humours would you say is most fashionable? Do you know anyone who seems to think that being depressed or melancholic makes him or her a more sensitive, a more soulful, a deeper, a more attractive, or a

more interesting person? Can you think of characters from popular movies, television shows, or books who could be characterized by the humours? How?

29. Rewrite the ending of *Romeo and Juliet*. Would this play be just as powerful if only one of the lead characters died? What other sorts of endings can you envision for this play? How would a different ending change the message of the play?

30. Add a new character to *Romeo and Juliet*. Give this character a name, a personality, good character traits, and character flaws. Give this character particular likes and dislikes. Create a background story, or "back story," for the character. Create some motivations or reasons to act for this character as well. What does this character want or desire? How does he or she think? What actions do they take?

Try writing some dialogue between this new character and at least one other character in the play. How does this change the play? Does it reveal anything new about a character we already know in the play?

31. Consider the ways *Romeo and Juliet* would be different if it were set in today's world. How would the technologies we use to communicate impact the play? How would Romeo and Juliet communicate with each other? Try translating the scene where Romeo and Juliet meet into a series of text messages. With all the instant technologies available to us today, how might the deaths of the two lovers still manage to take place. Being quarantined because of fears of the plague hardly works today.

32. How would today's mobile and diverse society change the play? In their time and place, Romeo and Juliet had few options or avenues for action available to them. What sorts of choices and courses of action are possible

today that just weren't at that time? On the other hand, are there modern dangers and obstacles that Romeo and Juliet would have to confront that might change the play?

33. What would happen if a couple of characters from *Romeo and Juliet* ran into or met a couple of characters from another Shakespeare play? What would Tybalt and Mercutio have to say to Brutus and Julius? What if Romeo met Hamlet and the two of them spent some time comparing their problems? What if Juliet and Ophelia found themselves talking about the difficulties they have with their lovers, Romeo and Hamlet? Would these characters learn anything from each other? Would it be a pleasant encounter, or would it be a disaster? What if Romeo and Juliet ran into the characters Lysander and Hermia from *A Midsummer Night's Dream*? Could they help each other out as they tried to overcome the obstacles in the way of their love? Would the characters learn something or grow in some way as a result of this encounter. Try writing a brief short story or dramatic scene that shows this encounter.

Film and *Romeo and Juliet*

Romeo and Juliet is an ever-popular play and continues to be staged frequently today. If at all possible, try to see an actual staged version of the play. These stage versions often present original interpretations of Shakespeare's play and can be of great use in interpreting the play and thinking about it in new ways. Many film versions of *Romeo and Juliet* also exist, ranging from silent film versions to animated cartoon versions of the play such as *Gnomeo and Juliet* directed by Kelly Asbury and released in 2011. The first film production of the play was produced in 1908: *Romeo and Juliet, A Romantic Story of the Ancient Feud Between the Italian Houses of Montague and Capulet*, directed by J. Stuart Blackston. A number of other silent versions of the film were produced, notably the 1924 film, *Romeo and Juliet*, in which the great Shakespearean actor, John Gielgud made his film debut.

"Talkie" (films with actors speaking their parts) versions of *Romeo and Juliet* began to appear in 1936 with George Cukor directing *Romeo and Juliet*, and continue to be produced today. A number of versions of *Romeo and Juliet* have also been produced for television. Three of the most interesting presentations and adaptations of the play are *Romeo + Juliet*, directed by Baz Lurhman (1996), *West Side Story* (1961), directed by Robert Wise and Jerome

Robbins, and *Romeo and Juliet* (1968), directed by Franco Zeffirelli.

Baz Luhrman's *Romeo + Juliet* is a fast-paced 1996 version the play set in Verona Beach in southern California and starring Leonardo DiCaprio and Claire Danes as Romeo and Juliet. Even the title stresses the contemporary dimension with its substitution of the "+" for "and." This "+" sign also puts a powerful emphasis on the adolescent quality of the two main characters with its echoes young love. Luhrman creates a great deal of spectacle in the film and uses this spectacle to contrast the intimate private nature of love with the power of the public image in our media-saturated culture. Throughout the film, clips of newscasters relating media versions of events along with spectacular images such as helicopters surrounding a giant statue of the Virgin Mary are interspersed with the more intimate scenes of the play. The sonnet that Shakespeare wrote as a prologue to the play is delivered by an anchorwoman who ends her narration by taking the audience to "live coverage" of the events of the play. This emphasis on media underscores just how important media is in contemporary culture and how difficult it can sometimes be to separate actual reality from the constructed images we are drenched with everyday.

This has been a very popular film version of the play, and some things about it work well, such as the preponderance of religious imagery, although this religious imagery isn't really linked to the "religion of love" that's so important in the play. The movie contains more of an assortment of images from Roman Catholicism. One way of thinking about the religious imagery in this film is to consider it as an updated version of the Petrarchanism Shakespeare uses throughout the play to develop a contrast between an idealized and false vision of love and the reality of love. The religious imagery Luhrman uses creates a sense of a false consciousness or lack of clear vision about reality in the same way that Petrarchanism does for Shakespeare and his original audience. In a sense this is an updating of the imagery of the play that works for an audience unfamiliar with Petrarch. The media images of a constructed, false reality do the same thing. *Romeo + Juliet* makes strong connections between the violence of much religious imagery, with its emphasis on sacrifice, suffering, and blood, and contemporary violence.This film also stresses the ganglike quality of the violence. It's fascinating to look at the ways Luhrman translated Renaissance themes and images into a contemporary setting. For instance the famous "Queen Mab" speech by Mercutio is delivered by a Mercutio dressed as a drag queen in a setting reminiscent of a rave.

The famous musical version of *Romeo and Juliet*, *West Side Story*, was produced on Broadway in 1957 and made into a popular film in 1961. The film stars Natalie Wood as "Juliet," named Maria Nuñez in the film, and Richard Beymer, as "Romeo," named Tony Wyzek in the film. *West Side Story* is set on the West Side of New York City and presents the play as the conflict between two rival gangs. One gang, the Jets, is made up of European Americans, and the other, the Sharks, is made up of Puerto Rican Americans. Throughout the musical the conflict and the feud is based upon the rivalries of these warring gangs rather than two warring families. The action of *West Side Story* is played out between these two rival gangs in New York rather than between two families feuding in Verona, Italy.

The musical stresses the tensions between different immigrant groups to the United States and the difficulty in overcoming the barriers raised by these conflicting immigrant cultures. The film also presents a contemporary version of the honor code and explores the theme of violence as a central component in American culture. The aesthetic quality of the songs and the dance numbers create a jarring contrast between an artistic experience and the actual nature and results of violence. The stylized quality of much of the violence underscores the difference between violence in real life and violence in art.

West Side Story does an excellent job of showing that tragedy often takes place among ordinary people—just as Shakespeare's play does.

The Franco Zeffirelli version of *Romeo and Juliet* (1968) is perhaps the classic adaptation of this play to film and is notable for its realism and its attempt to recreate the setting of the play with historical accuracy. Zeffirelli filmed the play in Pienza, Italy, a city in Tuscany which the United Nations has designated a World Historical Site. Pienza was designed by Pope Pius II who had the village of Corsignano rebuilt as an "ideal" renaissance town. Corsignano was the birthplace of Pope Pius II, and he had Pienze rebuilt to serve him as a retreat from Rome. The rebuilding was overseen by the Florentine (i.e., from Florence, Italy) architect Bernardo Ressellino and was conducted between 1459 and 1462. Today Pienza is often put forward as exactly what Pope Pius II hoped for—a stunning example of a Renaissance town. In addition to choosing Pienza as the location for filming this movie, Zeffirelli aimed for an accurate portrayal of the time period, including in the recreation of clothing and an accurate depiction of daily life during the period.

The film emphasizes the theme of conflict between generations—not surprising considering the importance of this issue in the 1960s and the growth of the counter culture movement at that time. The film also emphasizes the *carpe diem* or "seize the day" theme. The image of the rose figures prominently in this film, and Zeffirelli added a song about roses and the brevity of love to the film. A viewer familiar with this theme of *carpe diem* can hardly help recalling

Robert Herrick's famous Renaissance lyric, "To the Virgins to make much of Time," which opens with the lines,

> Gather ye rosebuds while ye may,
>
> Old Time is still a-flying:
>
> And this same flower that smiles to-day
>
> To-morrow will be dying.

The movie stars Leonard Whiting as Romeo and Olivia Hussy as Juliet. Both were young when the film was made. This was part of Zeffirelli's attempt at historical accuracy. As a director, Zeffirelli had no problem with cutting scenes and lines from the play or adding a song. Spend some time to thinking about how these alterations change the nature of the play and our experience of it. Adapting plays by cutting lines or scenes or by adding new material is a long-honored tradition in theater and film, and a contemporary audience should know that was just as true of Shakespeare's theatrical company as of a director in the twenty-first century.

Another screen version of *Romeo and Juliet* was released in 2013 under the title *Romeo & Juliet*. This version of the play was "adapted" by Julian Fellowes and directed by Carlo Carlei and stars Douglas Booth as Romeo and Hailee Steinfeld as Juliet. The film truly is an adaptation rather than a faithful presentation of Shakespeare's play. Although it is set in Italian locations, including Verona, the language has been modernized. Fellowes argues that the changes he made to Shakespeare's language are useful because, "to see the original in its absolutely unchanged form, you require a kind of Shakespearean scholarship, and you need to understand the language and analyze it and so on" (*New York Times*, October 11, 2013).

Many other versions of this play are available on DVD or from online streaming sites, ranging from the version directed by George Cukor in 1936 to the animated version *Gnomeo and Juliet.* Another film that touches on *Romeo and Juliet* is *Shakespeare in Love* (1998) with Gwyneth Paltrow and Ben Affleck. It's always fun to compare different film versions of the play since this can provide insights into how different people have thought of the play as well as showing how different generations have stressed different aspects of the play.

Suggestions for Further Reading and Exploration

Shakespeare has had more critical attention directed toward him than any other English-language writer. This brief annotated bibliography suggests only a few titles for each section, but these are books that will help expand your knowledge of Shakespeare and his time if you would like to pursue the study of Shakespeare in more depth.

Backgrounds to the Elizabeth Age and Shakespeare's Worldview

Kermode, Frank. *The Age of Shakespeare*. New York: The Modern Library. 2005. This is a relatively short and accessible introduction to Shakespeare's time. Kermode uses fascinating detail about the period to keep the reader engaged as he presents both the Elizabethan and Jacobean eras and explores the theatrical world in which Shakespeare lived and worked.

Tillyard, E. M.W. *The Elizabethan World Picture*. New York: Vintage books, 1959. This is an older book, but it's short and provides a good overview of some of the basic ideas that determined the ways

Shakespeare and his contemporaries approached the world.

Biographies

Bate, Jonathan. *Soul of the Age: A Biography of the Mind of William Shakespeare*. New York: Random House, 2010. Bate presents Shakespeare as being, in many ways, typical of the Elizabethan age. He explores Shakespeare's careers as an actor, playwright, and poet, and places him squarely in the context of Elizabethan England as he explores such topics as Shakespeare's reading and education and their influence on his plays.

Greenblatt, Stephen. *Will in the World: How Shakespeare Became Shakespeare*. New York: W.W. Norton, 2004. Greenblatt presents an engrossing story of Shakespeare's life but also gives a detailed portrait of the culture of Shakespeare's time and the world in which he lived. Greenblatt explores Shakespeare's relationships with other writers and such topics as the possible relationships between events in Shakespeare's life such as the death of his son Hamnet and his plays. Greenblatt is particularly strong at capturing the culture of Shakespeare's time. This is a biography of the Elizabethan and Jacobean ages as well as a biography of Shakespeare.

Shapiro, James. *A Year in the Life of William Shakespeare: 1599*. New York: Harper Perennial, 2006. Shapiro chooses to focus on one year in the life of Shakespeare, and it was a crucial year. This is the year that saw the opening of The Globe Theatre as well as the production of *Henry V*, *Julius Caesar*, and *As You Like it*. Shapiro also includes the possibility of *Hamlet* as a production of this year. Shapiro captures the slippery political world Shakespeare had to negotiate as a writer and creates a fascinating portrait of Shakespeare and his age.

Many other excellent biographies address Shakespeare and his life and times. The second edition of Samuel Schoenbaum's outstanding book, *Shakespeare's Lives* published by Oxford University Press in 1993, traces the history of biographies of Shakespeare from the eighteenth century to the present. He also includes the basic information that Shakespeare biographers use to create their biographies and a variety of legends that have accumulated around Shakespeare. This book is aimed at the academic reader, but is fascinating for anyone interested in Shakespeare and how he has been perceived at different times. Charles Nicholl's, *The Lodger Shakespeare: His Life on Silver Street*, published by Viking in 2007 is an excellent book that explores the world of Shakespeare in 1603-1605 when he was a lodger in a household that was later part of a lawsuit for which Shakespeare had to give a deposition. Don't let the subject mater fool you—this is a worthwhile read.

Critical studies

Literally thousands of critical studies have been written about Shakespeare and his works, and many of these are well done. Here is a handful of the most useful books for the general reader interested in Shakespeare.

Garber, Marjorie. *Shakespeare After All*. New York: Pantheon Books, 2004. Garber has written a number of excellent and interesting critical studies on Shakespeare, and in this book she offers an introduction to Shakespeare and then presents detailed and thoughtful essays on each of Shakespeare's plays. These essays are brilliant analyses of the individual play and help guide the reader through some of the complexities of each play. Garber is a clear writer and manages to mostly stay away from the jargon that often accompanies literary criticism. This is an accessible but scholarly introduction to Shakespeare and his plays.

Kermode, Frank. *Shakespeare's Language*. New York: Farrar, Straus and Giroux, 2000. Kermode's book is an accessible exploration of Shakespeare's language. He explores the changes that took place in Shakespeare's use of language after 1600, although he also writes about Shakespeare's language before that year. This work is written in a straightforward style and is directed toward the general reader interested in Shakespeare and the way Shakespeare used language with such extraordinary effect.

McAlindon, Thomas. *Shakespeare's Tragic Cosmos*. Cambridge: Cambridge University Press, 1996. McAlindon's book is a wonderful corrective to the traditional view of the Elizabethans and Jacobeans that stressed such things as the Great Chain of Being and a view of the universe as harmonious. McAlindon emphasizes that the Elizabethans actually had two views of the universe: one based on harmony and the other on disharmony or contraries. He puts Shakespeare's work into a context of these competing forces and uses this opposition to present clear and thoughtful analyses of the tragedies.

Rosenbaum, Ron. *The Shakespeare Wars: Clashing Scholars, Public Fiascoes, Palace Coups*. New York: Random House, 2006. Rosenbaum's book is an interesting exploration of a variety of the controversies in current Shakespeare studies. He is particularly interested in questions about how Shakespeare should be printed and performed. This book gets a bit heavy on detail at times but opens the world of Shakespeare Studies and some of its important questions to the general reader.

Shapiro, James. *Contested Will: Who Wrote Shakespeare?* New York: Simon and Schuster, 2010. Shapiro digs into the question of "who wrote Shakespeare" in this book and tries to understand why so many people have questioned whether Shakespeare was the actual author of the plays attributed to him. Shapiro manages to make this controversy come alive for the contemporary reader, and Shapiro makes the case powerfully and clearly that Shakespeare did, indeed, write all of the plays he is credited with writing.

Web Resources

A number of excellent websites are devoted to Shakespeare, Shakespeare Studies, and the individual plays. Here's a listing of some of the most useful of the many websites available.

http://www.shakespeare-navigators.com

http://www.folger.edu

http://www.shakespeare.mit.edu

http://www.shakespeare-online.com

We hope that this *Make It Fun Guide to Romeo and Juliet* has helped you to know Shakespeare and his play, *Romeo and Juliet*, better. Each time you read or watch this play, or any other Shakespeare play, try to be actively engaged in the reading or viewing experience. If you bring an active mind to Shakespeare, each reading or viewing of his work will help deepen your understanding into Shakespeare and his works.

Shakespeare wrote to connect with his audience. He wanted to entertain his audience and to lead them to deeper reflection. We hope that you are touched by his work as countless others have been before you. Have fun with Shakespeare and his works. After all, these are "plays."

Larry K. Hartsfield is a professor of English and Environmental Studies at Fort Lewis College in Durango, Colorado where he teaches Shakespeare, Environmental Literature, the history of the novel, and a variety of courses in American Literature. Professor Hartsfield has won awards for excellence in teaching at his college and has been recognized as the undergraduate teacher of the year for the Colorado State University System. He received his Ph.D. in American Civilization at the University of Texas at Austin. In addition to *The Make It Fun Guide to Romeo and Juliet*, he is the author of *The Make It Fun Guide to Poetry*, *A Journey to Health: Overcoming Inflammatory Bowel Disease*, and *The American Response to Professional Crime, 1870-1917*.

www.ingramcontent.com/pod-product-compliance
Lightning Source LLC
Chambersburg PA
CBHW060506030426
42337CB00015B/1756